THE COURAGE TO FIGHT BACK

"How much do you make?" There was an edge to Joy's voice, a hard edge rarely heard.

"Five-ninety-two." Joy was her friend. They worked together. Why shouldn't she know?

"I make five-fifty. Karon, I've been a nurse for more than ten years. I went to school for this. I paid to learn this business. I have to deal with a lot of nasty stuff at work. Sometimes, I even save lives. And I earn the same as some 16-year-old kid who works the cash register at National Star. I don't understand it. I honestly don't understand what's going on, I . . ." And her voice trailed off. She sat for a moment with her head down and her hands clenched, then she looked up.

"Can you figure this out? Do you know what's wrong?"

Karon shook her head. "We're getting screwed, that's all I can tell you. We are getting screwed."

"AN INSPIRING TRUE STORY OF TWO COURAGEOUS WOMEN WILLING TO FIGHT FOR THEIR IDEALS."
Chattanooga Times

Nurses:

ON OUR OWN

**KARON WHITE GIBSON, R.N.,
JOY SMITH CATTERSON, R.N.
AND PATRICIA SKALKA**

AN AUTHORS GUILD BACKINPRINT.COM EDITION

Nurses:
On Our Own

AN AUTHORS GUILD BACKINPRINT.COM EDITION

Published by iUniverse.com, Inc.

For information address:
iUniverse.com, Inc.
5220 S 16th, Ste. 200
Lincoln, NE 68512
www.iuniverse.com

Originally published by St. Martin's Press

The events here are true, but for reasons of privacy,
the names of patients, medical personnel and medical institutions have been changed.

ISBN: 0-595-14362-8

Printed in the United States of America

Acknowledgments: in appreciation to Raymond J. Padvoiskis, Fernando A. Lopez, MD, Barbara Bolsen, and Leslie M. Pockell. Each in their own way contributed to making this story possible.

Cover photos by Ralph Gibson

KWG: To Ralph, who believed in and encouraged me, and to my nieces, Spring and Carisa, with the hope that life presents greater options to them as women.

JSC: To my family: Gordon, Debbie, Kathy, John, and Jimmy.

And for our colleague nurses: to inspire the reluctant, to celebrate the activist, to exult the independent.

nurses:

on
our
own

chapter one

*T*he city was hot that Monday morning, even at dawn. High up in the atmosphere, wide ribbons of cool air moved easily back and forth over the metropolitan area, but down close to the ground a stagnant pollution leaned against the people and buildings of Chicago. For three days there had been little wind, and the heat, like a shroud made visible by trapped particles and fluffs of dust, settled itself into backyards, parks, cemeteries, any bit of open space. Soon the temperature rose still higher, as the sun's glow touched Lake Michigan with a blinding white light. Then, almost instantaneously, it was upon the land, tumbling over the city's beaches and steel mills, bombarding the tall green trees and thick shrubs that ringed the suburban mansions to the north. As the sunlight moved silently west, old men selling early editions of the *Chicago Tribune* and *Sun-Times* on street corners wiped their arms, sweaty with newsprint, across their foreheads. At the city's bus terminals, drivers pulled sticking pants away from their legs and reluctantly climbed aboard green and white buses that would soon turn into rolling ovens. Moment by moment the city woke up, cursing the heat and trying to beat it. But for most people it was already too late. It was that kind of day.

On the city's South Side, Joy Catterson tossed a basket full of baby and toddler clothes into her automatic washer, glancing out the utility room window at her husband backing his car out of the garage. She watched him without emotion or interest, as one would watch a traffic light change color. It was seven o'clock in the morning. Gordon, a policeman, was going to work. Joy had the kids to feed and house to clean before leaving for her own job that

1

afternoon. She had planned to go to the grocery store and to stop by at a friend's to roll up her hair, but then decided to stay home because of the heat. Now with her long auburn-brown hair brushed back into a pony tail and wearing one of her husband's tee shirts and a pair of cut-off jeans, Joy set herself up in the family room with her two young daughters, aged two and five, the first load of laundry to be folded, the television, and the air conditioner.

Joy, 28, had grown up in Chicago. As a child her home had been nearer the lake, but she and her family had moved farther and farther out as neighborhoods changed and populations shifted. Joy had never had a house before and enjoyed the feeling of space and independence this one gave her. When she was inside, it didn't bother her so much that the home she and Gordon had worked so hard for looked just like the two to the right and the two to the left of them, five three-bedroom yellow brick trilevels on a street of white and yellow brick houses. It was an ordinary street, in an ordinary neighborhood, on a hot but otherwise ordinary day in June, 1968.

At eleven o'clock Joy went into the kitchen to make lunch. Just about that time, 12 miles away, in a pale orange-and-white bedroom an alarm clock sounded and Joy's coworker Karon White struggled awake. Karon's heavy curtains were pulled tight against the day, and the light that filtered into the room played upon soft heaps of clothes: double paneled slip, white uniform, and nylons lay scattered across the 14-foot horizon. Slowly a tall, slender figure entered the scene, rising up from beneath a thin yellow sheet and groping for a misplaced robe. She sat a moment there on the edge of the bed, then stepped quickly to the white wooden French door. On the other side was the rest of the two-bedroom, two-bath, shag-carpeted suburban apartment she shared with another young woman, a former classmate and friend.

Karon left for work first. At two o'clock she hurried from the cool of the apartment to the air-conditioned 1964 Buick parked in the lot behind the building. Five minutes later she sat in relative comfort and cautiously edged the bulky red convertible to the street, checking her soles for tar stains as she waited for a break in traffic. If the shoes weren't completely clean, she'd have to repolish them when she got to work. Nice change from the ghetto, Karon thought, as she moved through the traffic of a busy commercial street. Nice finally to be done with school and training and to be part of the real world.

Karon was almost at the door of her work place when Joy Catterson, hair straight and makeup fresh, stepped out of her back door and walked past her husband, the babysitter, who was coming home for the afternoon. From the alley to the street to the expressway, mechanically she rode past the familiar houses and stores. Joy liked to drive. She enjoyed the sensation of moving, the excitement of a changing scene. As a child she had loved the long rides to Wisconsin for fishing vacations with her parents and brother, and even now, if she could, Joy would leave on a moment's notice for anyplace within a day's drive. There were many times she regretted not having the chance. Two forty-five. Right on schedule, Joy punched the top elevator button, 7E, rode the lift up, and was buzzed into her special work area.

"Good afternoon, good afternoon, hello, hello," she chanted, smiling to the small cluster of people inside. Joy was not aware of the solid heavy thump of the door's steel lock that echoed quietly behind her. A sound that had haunted her initially had become indiscernible from its surroundings. The lock became irrelevant when you had the key to get out.

This was the psych ward, General Community Hospital, Chicago. Thirty patients on the inside, a potential six million on the outside. Below were floor upon floor of white, adjustable beds filled with people with physically ill bodies. But here, separated from the rest of the world, locked out or in, were those with the bruised minds and spirits. In one way or another, and to varying degrees, they had either lost contact with or lost the ability to deal with reality. Here, in their own private space, they were given time to rest and to recover from their wounds. This was their

3

refuge, albeit a temporary one, a sanctuary for those who could no longer cope. During the Middle Ages a fugitive or debtor could find sanctuary in the cathedral for 40 days; psych patients could stay in the ward three months. At that time those who were either improved or cured went home; the others were almost inevitably doomed to further institutionalization at a private or state mental facility.

Private psych wards are not the babbling, hectic zoos most people imagine. For all their problems, the patients tend to act relatively normal most of the time. What must be watched for, however, are those moments when their tenuous control fails. Thus the locked door; the basic staff rule that you never turn your back on a psych patient; the nightly room checks for mirrors, rattail combs, scissors, any objects that can be used to inflict harm; and the precut shower curtain rods in all the bathrooms, guaranteed to break immediately under the weight of a hanging body. There are no straitjackets on psych wards anymore, but there are temporary restraints, heavy brown leather belts attached to the sides of the bed frames, which, when needed, lash down limbs in an order prescribed by state law: left arm, right leg or right arm, left leg. On rare occasions all four straps are used and a fifth added across the torso, but a patient is never strapped face down, a posture the law considers inhumane and dangerous.

This ward, more than others, is a place where the sick and the well, the patients and the healers, live every day in an atmosphere of uneasy peace, waiting for the truce to be broken. At first the tension itself is maddening, then, as with the click of the steel door, you get used to it.

Karon White, RN, was the charge nurse on the ward during the second shift, the three to 11 run. Only six months before, Karon had graduated from nursing school and taken her first job at another hospital, where she worked both the emergency room and the psych ward. Then she applied for a position at General, which was just setting up its psychiatric unit. Later she heard that another woman had already been selected to be in charge, but when Karon arrived, she was given the job. She was only 22, energetic, and full of ideas. Making good meant a lot to Karon. She moved into her slot eagerly, confidently. She wanted nothing more than to work hard and prove that she was more than a good nurse, that she was an excellent nurse.

For Joy Smith Catterson, RN, nursing was just a job, though the psych ward presented a new, exciting experience. Joy had been a medical-surgical nurse for seven years, and each year had further dimmed the original dream, until what had begun as dedication to an ideal became simply a means to a paycheck. She was a highly competent nurse in a technical sense, but knew that in a more important way she had been a better one when she had started. She had lost some of her enthusiasm, but she accepted this as inevitable and now just took each day as it came. She tried not to think too far into the future and made no career plans, so there could be no disappointment.

Eventually, Karon and Joy would become much more than simply coworkers. In addition to becoming close friends they would strike out together on a new venture that would totally alter their lives. None of this was apparent to them that afternoon, however. They were too busy with patients, too preoccupied with the oppressive heat.

The psych ward was almost brand new. Despite the air conditioning now going full blast, many of the patients complained. One of the thirty on 7E was a young black woman, a former high school biology teacher who for no discernible reason had one day put a gun to her temple and tried to blow off her head. Something had gone wrong and she hadn't died as she had wanted. Instead, Aldine, who had been beautiful and outgoing, became withdrawn and sullen. Her family, bowing before what they felt was their failure to help their sister and daughter, had transferred her from a medical unit to the psych ward.

Aldine sat in the dayroom in front of the television, silent, her eyes staring at the floor. She turned her head only once when Karon White entered the room. The nurse was trying to get the patient more involved with activities on the floor. "Want to sit by the door?" she asked. "You can watch the visitors come in." Aldine was silent—at least she offered no protest.

So they came down the hallway together, the young black woman slumped over in a wheelchair, the tall young nurse pushing her, quickly, efficiently, because that was the way she liked to do things.

Three feet from the station, Karon stopped, turned the portable chair toward the locked entrance, and set the brake.

"Is this all right?" she asked, polite but crisp, not really expecting an answer. In the next thirty minutes, Karon completed nurse's notes on ten patient charts, wrote two admission histories, answered five phone calls from doctors, and buzzed in at least half a dozen visitors. Karon liked being in charge and wasn't afraid of the responsibility that came with the position. "Witch in White" some patients called her, partly because her birthday fell on Halloween, partly because of her long jet-black hair that shimmered almost blue against the stark white of the uniform and the paler tones of her face.

Karon had just finished charting, the sound of the metal trays distinct in the quiet haze of the afternoon, when suddenly she heard a laugh, a low guttural murmur, almost a snicker, coming from Aldine. Karon may have been young, but already she knew to be wary. You don't ignore the signs, not any of them, she said to herself, as she slid off the chair. In five long, quiet steps she was out of the nurses' station and alongside the wheelchair.

Her body taut and ready to spring, Karon froze, momentarily stunned. Once, as a student nurse, she had had to attend to the labor and delivery of a 13-year-old girl pregnant from an uncle's rape. On her first job, she'd had to deal with a homosexual man who insisted on parading through the ward in the nude, and had had to defend two orderlies from a sexual assault charge brought by a former patient. Karon thought she had seen it all. Now she knew she hadn't.

Aldine had her hospital gown lifted to the shoulders, exposing

6

her entire naked body. Her legs were draped over the sides of the wheelchair, and she sat in full view of the visitor's window and entrance, masturbating. Some movement must have alerted Aldine to Karon's presence because she turned an expressionless face toward the nurse, and without a word withdrew her finger and slipped it into her mouth.

"Oh my God, Aldine, how could you? I could murder you!" Karon hadn't moved. All her energy and force went into those few words, which came slowly and hung heavily in the air. The next instant the scene was one of pandemonium. Karon ordered repeatedly, "Stop it. Stop it." She grappled for a hold, jumped back as Aldine's legs sprang viciously out, lunged forward again, trying to shove the patient's arm up and her gown down as visitors congregated outside the door, peeking in. Again Aldine kicked. Each time the nurse stepped closer, Aldine smirked and whipped her long, skinny arms forward, waving her nails in Karon's face. For what seemed longer than the few seconds that actually passed, they stood each other off until Karon used her one advantage. She could move faster on her feet than Aldine could in the wheelchair. Like a Keystone Kop, she ran the ten short steps that put her behind the patient. She had Aldine pinned down by the shoulders when Joy arrived to help. Together they wheeled the patient back to her room and secured her in restraints, not as a punishment but as a control for her antisocial behavior. Aldine said nothing as she lay flat on her back, while the heavy brown leather belts were attached. Her eyes were closed and she refused to acknowledge the two nurses who worked quickly around her.

Karon slammed the door on the way out. "That little creep. She knew exactly what she was doing. She's not crazy. She knew. God, I'm so embarrassed. I hope those visitors don't think that was going on all afternoon."

Joy was quiet. She thought Karon was too easily shocked but she said nothing. Karon was the boss, younger, but still had the last word on the unit.

In many ways, large and small, Joy Catterson and Karon White were different. The contrast in appearance and temperament were most striking. Karon was taller and more forceful in her actions; she rarely smiled and sometimes seemed aloof and distant. Joy was shy and the gentler of the two. She'd smile and flash her brown eyes and laugh off a problem or incident that would have Karon consumed for hours. Now as they walked down the hall together, Joy began talking about another patient, drawing Karon's attention away from Aldine. Joy thought Karon needed to learn to bend a little, Karon wanted Joy to learn to fight back and to speak out.

Once, in nursing school, Joy had been assertive and had told a woman patient about her scheduled surgery. The next day Joy was reprimanded because the woman had cancelled the upcoming hysterectomy. "You shouldn't have told the patient about the nature of the surgery," Joy was told. "But legally I'm supposed to," she argued back.

Since then Joy had been the model nurse, pushed to the extreme only one time when she gambled with her license to save a man's life. She was the night duty nurse at a small hospital that had no physicians on call. When the patient, an elderly man with diabetes, went into insulin shock, she spent precious minutes telephoning, trying to get permission to medicate the patient. Then she did what no nurse should ever do without an MD's direct order: she drew up the indicated medication and walked through the dim corridor ready to give the injection. Like a small miracle, a doctor appeared around the corner. He was there completely by chance, he said, making a late-night visit to a patient. When Joy stopped him, the physician, who happened to be an obstetrician, gave her the okay to prepare the syringe she already carried in her hand. He knew nothing about the case but he carried the authority to prescribe. The next day Joy reported the incident to the administration, pointing to the need to have a doctor stationed on the premises 24 hours a day, but her comments were ignored. Joy thought of the incident now as she walked back to the station with Karon. She tried to imagine Karon in that situation.

8

With Aldine in restraints, the floor returned to normal. Patients went back to their televisions and magazines, while Joy and another nurse heated the individual dinner trays in the ward's microwave oven. The meal was quiet; even the middle-aged lady who periodically accused the staff of piping mustard gas into her room behaved.

Later, medications were given and at nine o'clock Joy and Agnes, a quiet, veteran nurse who kept her mentally ill husband locked in the basement because she couldn't afford psychiatric care for him, took their one-to-one's off to quiet corners of the ward for a twice-weekly talk. Most of the other patients congregated by the unit's three color televisions sets while six select men and women traipsed into the dayroom after Karon for the current events series she had introduced a month before, with the approval of the administration and the patients' psychiatrists.

When the door closed behind them, Karon the nurse became Karon the teacher, assigning articles from the morning paper to a class of disoriented learners. Each patient read one story, then summarized it for the group. They were hesitant and embarrassed. These were the most solitary, withdrawn patients, the ones who had drifted furthest from everyday reality, who seldom spoke or heard what was said to them. The current events class was an attempt to break through their individual barriers and to pour a little of the outside world into their private universes. For one hour, twice a week, they huddled around the familiar white formica table and made feeble contact with each other, reading and rereading sentence by sentence, trying to comprehend the articles.

Finally, at ten, Karon returned to the nurses' station, flipped on the intercom, and told all patients to go to their rooms for room check.

"Go to hell," an anonymous voice boomed back. "We want to watch TV."

Karon turned to one of the orderlies. "Go ahead," the signal to start the room checks. "Catterson, find Willis and do the check tonight. Sorry."

9

Gwen Willis, everyone agreed, was proof either of how desperate for nurses the hospital was or how little the administration cared about anything but the RN after the name. Gwen was incompetent, unpersonable, and sloppy. No one kept track of the bets any longer about the last time Gwen had taken a bath or washed her hair or changed her uniform. Shortly after Karon was hired she had reported the young nurse for lack of professionalism, but her supervisor had ignored the complaint and Gwen, who raised cats, continued to show up for duty with smudges of black dirt on her clothing and a thick body odor hanging over her.

Now Joy pinched her nostrils together with her left hand and backed out of the station, bowing as she went. She knew room check was important because it gave the staff a chance to locate contraband and to make a final evaluation of patient moods for the night. But it was still a wretched task, shuffling through patients' dirty socks and personal belongings, emptying waste baskets, like garbage collectors, with the orderlies. "It isn't in our job descriptions," they complained. "It isn't in mine either," Joy replied. She hadn't been told about moments like this in nursing school.

There was little else to do that evening. Karon made one last check on Aldine, and rather than disturb her decided to leave her in restraints until the next shift. Finally she went into the conference room to tape her daily report, as charge nurse. At 11:15, just as she and Joy were leaving, one of the two hall pay phones rang. Five, six, seven times it bleated tinny and hollow in the small empty area by the nurses' station. Finally Joy picked up the receiver, mocking the insistent nasal voice that demanded she deposit five more cents. They got these calls at least three times a week, one for every toll call made by Emily, a grandmotherly patient whose only vice was her periodic highly active manic states. Emily never had enough money for any of the calls she made and she always ran off before the operators called back.

"Lady," said Joy, her voice suddenly droll, "I don't have a nickel. The person who made the call does not have nickel either. This is the psych ward of a hospital."

10

"I must have another five cents. Put the nickel in."

"You put the nickel in!" Joy hung up.

On the elevator she turned to Karon. "Do you think the operator believed me, about the psych ward?"

"Would you?" The answer was almost lost in the click of the closing doors.

On the first floor the nurses turned left, walked past the deserted front lobby and out the side door where a few scattered street lights marked the way to the parking lot. Doctors used the well-lit main entrance to the hospital but nurses, unless they took the bus, could not. When someone mentioned security, they were told it was a safe neighborhood and warned not to cause trouble.

There was something satisfying about the hospital late at night, something both Karon and Joy felt. The building was strength standing in the moonlight, its awkward modern dimensions softened by the darkness. What looked cold and garish by day was almost mystical at night, here where life and death so often passed each other in the halls. Inside, people like Karon and Joy were joined in common purpose. Outside they went their separate ways.

Joy was the homemaker, the mother. She shook out throw rugs from the back door, waxed her kitchen floor, read stories to her children, clipped coupons from the Thursday food section of the paper, and read mysteries at night. She existed from day to day, moving from her kitchen to her neighbor's kitchen, hurrying from a child's dancing lesson to a pile of dirty laundry. It wasn't an exciting life but it was a busy one, with a husband, job, children. Beyond Gordon's drinking, Joy could find nothing really wrong with her life. Everyone she knew lived as she did. As long as the bills were paid, the family was clothed, there was food on the table, and every month or so a party or wedding to attend, where the others laughed so hard at Gordon's jokes that tears streamed down their faces, then they had nothing to complain about.

What Joy did that summer was what she had done every summer of her marriage. Two days a week—it had been five at one time—she dressed in white: long white slip, white stockings, white shoes, white dress, and white cap, and went off to empty bedpans, pass medications, stop nosebleeds, and watch in dismay as her medical acumen slowly dissolved. She tried to tell Gordon about it, how frustrating it was to be tied down and limited when she knew she could do so much more. He said she should be glad she wasn't responsible for the really hard decisions, that she had enough to take care of in her life. "Let the doctors worry about all that," he said. "They get paid more than you, anyway. Just do your job and come home." Joy hadn't discussed much about work after that.

As for the rest of her time, it just seemed to slip past her. When she and Gordon were first married, Joy had discovered that dwelling on problems only made them worse. How many hours she'd cried over his drinking, how many nights she'd waited up for him, then stood screaming at him from the foot of the bed when he'd finally tumbled through the door, disgusted with herself for doing to Gordon what her mother had done to her father. None of it made any difference, though. None of her plotting or planning or pleading had gotten anywhere, so she withdrew and became passive.

Joy learned to play checkers with her life, unthinkingly moving objects from one square to another to take the place of something that suddenly was eliminated from the board. She moved children and friends onto the square Gordon was supposed to occupy, moved her mother from the shadows onto the front row space her father had occupied until his death. Eight months later, her mother died and Joy turned again to Gordon. That hadn't worked and by midsummer Joy, only vaguely aware of emptiness, began actively thinking of babies, asking Gordon if he wouldn't want a son, knowing his pride insisted on one and that her next pregnancy was only matter of time.

Joy's game of checkers extended even to work. After seven years she finally had to admit to herself that she was bored. Nursing had seemed to offer so much but had fallen short of her

12

expectations. She took orders, that was all, and for the privilege practically had to pay with her soul for a job that was becoming spiritually empty and financially unrewarding. This new sense of emptiness was forming, just about the time a new person came into her life, someone with enough energy, nerve, and innocent determination to distract her and help fill the void. Mentally, Joy already equated the two: nursing and new boss. When she thought hospital she often, in her mind's eye, saw Karon. At least Karon wasn't boring and Joy, who liked to live vicariously, found herself more and more drawn to this other woman, one so unlike the rest of the people in her sphere.

If there are those who feel cheated by life because they were not born with enough confidence and willpower, it could be because people like Karon got more than a normal share. In the 1960s it would probably have been fair to say that Karon had the qualities most parents would want in a son: to believe oneself capable of anything; to be assertive, strong, and just idealistic enough to think you alone could make a difference. It would probably be more accurate to say Karon had led the kind of sheltered life that had allowed her to be all these things, and so to assume she could continue doing so indefinitely.

Karon's mother, a quiet, conservative housewife, and her father, an executive for an insurance company, had built a strong fortress for their daughter. She had had freedom, but within strict bounds. She had had responsibility for decisions but only when the choices were clearly defined. Consequently, there were no grays in Karon's life. People were either good or bad, something was either right or wrong. Extentuating circumstances didn't exist. When a doctor hung up the phone on her because she questioned a medication dosage, Karon responded the only way she knew how. During their next conversation, she hung up on him, later explaining she would do this again every time he did it to her. There was no lack of respect for him as a professional—just a healthy dose of respect for her own professional status.

But of much in life she was terribly naive. Karon's parents had taught her that honesty and pride were the jewels of life, but they did not tell her about the dishonest people, the ones who lacked pride and had lost their integrity in some dark corner or to some easy deal. When Karon met blatant examples she was repelled, stymied. When she saw them in disguise, she failed at first to recognize their true nature.

At 19 she had fallen in love with a deceitful man because she could not imagine anyone lying about something as basic as being married. When she found out Brian had a wife and a new baby, she turned on the tall, handsome policeman, with his laughing blue eyes and easy strong wit. She hated him so much she became physically ill and withdrew to bed for three weeks. As much as she despised him, Karon detested herself even more for being so gullible, so stupid. Scarred and angry, she spent two years dating and rejecting men.

Brian had soured her on policemen, so Karon turned to the men around her. Medical students, she thought, should be exciting. But they weren't, nor was the dental student she dated for a while. Never had Karon encountered such egotistical, demanding men, who flippantly expected sexual favors as a matter of course and treated women like footstools. They were cheap too, she decided, playing the role of the poor student, even the ones who had money. Karon was finally cured of dating doctors the evening she sat for eight and a half hours waiting for the chief cardiac resident to come out of surgery to take her to the biggest party of the season. How can you get mad at a man who's late because he's saving someone's life? she wondered. You can't, but that doesn't make missing the party any easier.

Karon was back dating cops again when she met Ralph, a man all her fine rules militated against. Ralph was divorced, and according to her strict white/black standards should have been an evilhearted louse. On top of that, Ralph was a playboy and Karon wasn't accustomed to the competition. For months she spied on him, tailed him, double-checked his every word and action, jealously guarding her own heart from the pain she knew he could

14

inflict. Karon set out to prove to herself that Ralph was a bastard and ended up having to rethink her rules and falling in love with him.

It was Ralph she slipped in next to that evening after she left the hospital, opening the door to the new yellow Ford and sliding across the seat to kiss him.

"God," she said throwing her arms into the air. "It's been one of those nights. Let's get dinner and a drink."

Nonstop she went through the events of the day. Karon liked to talk. Ralph had discovered this on their first date when she kept going hours past midnight. Now he listened easily to her chatter. He was 32 years old, had been through a bad marriage and every day on the job, his policeman's gun strapped to his hip, came in contact with at least one rotten example of life gone wrong. People called him "pig" and he'd learned to keep quiet. People shot at him and he'd had to learn to shoot back. The worst time had been when Ralph was on the police TASK Force. A wave of gang crime was sweeping the west side and someone had come at him from behind a tall stand of hedges, holding a rifle at the ready. The gunman ignored Ralph's warning to drop his weapon, and Ralph had no choice but to shoot, though he aimed not at the kill zone but at the suspect's right leg. Ralph ran to the spot where the gunman had fallen and stopped, horrified, as he looked down into the face of a 16-year-old boy. "My God, it's just a kid," he said.

Later, Ralph moved on to more exotic pursuits, donning a long blonde wig and babushka to become a decoy in a drive to deter crime against women. With his badge and gun tucked into a black patent-leather purse, Ralph spent many nights standing in darkened doorways and loitering at bus and train stations, trying to look helpless, playing the role of potential victim.

But Ralph wasn't thinking about any of that now. He had a child support payment due at the end of the week and a dispute to settle with some other cops over their jointly owned power boat, moored in one of the city's lakefront harbors. With half his attention, Ralph thought of these things; with the other half he followed Karon's litany. Familiar names and faces came into focus. He barely heard something about an incident with some nameless patient that day but Karon talked too fast for much of it to make sense.

Ralph marveled at this woman, at her energy, her quick intelligence and stubborn dedication to her job. Part of being a cop, it seemed, was being exposed to hospitals. You brought in wounded suspects, dead victims, and too often, your own fellow policemen, shot up and frightened and trying not to admit it. You had to be nice to the nurses because you never knew when you might be flat on your back looking up into the face of someone to whom you'd just issued a parking ticket. The emergency room of the local hospital soon became as familiar as the front office of your station. No wonder so many policemen dated and eventually married nurses. They understood each other, they knew about working strange hours, about reacting under stress, about being alone and apprehensive, about being villains and heroes. All of them dealt, in one way or another, with death and the less pleasant side of people and life, and they turned naturally to each other for comfort or a laugh, for some reassurance of normalcy in their lives.

Ralph knew a lot of nurses and a lot of women, but he knew no one quite like Karon. At first he'd been amused by her strict, no nonsense code of ethics: no going alone to a boyfriend's apartment, no staying at parties where there's open necking. Then he'd been annoyed; none of the usual little rewards were there. He could get further with a virtual stranger than with this woman he'd dated for months. Finally he accepted her. He realized Karon wasn't going to change and that the decision was his. He could stick it out or drop her, and in the end, he knew, he wouldn't mind having her in his corner.

Ralph wondered sometimes what made Karon so suspicious and guarded. Something her mother had ingrained in her, something that had happened to a friend, something that had happened to her? She responded to men like an animal once caught in a human trap, with consummate distrust. For a few weeks after

16

he'd told her about his previous marriage, Karon had fluctuated wildly in her moods. One minute she was almost gleeful, triumphant that her worst fears had been realized. Minutes later she was subdued, as if she really cared for him and was struggling to accept his past. Ralph knew eventually she would get back at him and she did. One day, infuriated that other women phoned him at his apartment, Karon called the phone company. She identified herself as Mrs. Ralph Gibson, complained about some obscene phone calls, and asked for a new number, effective immediately. For two weeks Karon gloated. No one but she could call Ralph. The day the new number notice arrived in the mail, the game was up.

Ralph looked at her incredulously. "What do you call this?" he asked waving the envelope in her face.

He expected an excuse, a denial; instead, he got a straightforward, honest answer. That afternoon he loaned her the keys to his new car.

By the summer Karon was working at General, she felt certain Ralph was the man she would marry, but she was in no hurry. They saw each other almost every day and talked three or four times daily on the phone. He'd met her parents and brothers and she'd met his daughter. Eventually they started talking the way potential married couples talk, about the kind of summer house they both wanted one day, about places to vacation together, about whether to have children. That summer was one of the best for Karon. She had what she wanted most, the things she'd always thought meant happiness. She'd always dreamed of being a nurse and she was one. She had Ralph. She went out almost every night, if not with him, then with friends. She had money to spend. It was not unusual for Karon to leave $200 in a bureau drawer, just lying there, giving her a sense of independence. She couldn't believe how easy life was and couldn't imagine that it would get anything but better.

Then barefoot, ragged people started throwing bags of feces and urine around the streets of Chicago and larger realities took the stage as the 1968 Democratic National Convention opened and the "Days of Rage" began. The Yippies who invaded the city from across the country were trying to make a point. but to judge by the response on 7E, they failed completely. These people, staff and patients alike, were too far removed in every sense to sympathize or to see the larger picture. Their values and lifestyles were threatened by the actions of the few and they resented it bitterly. Joy, who hadn't been feeling well lately, was relieved that at least Gordon was kept on in the neighborhood.

For Karon it was worse. Ralph was down at the lakefront, in the front lines of helmeted police battling the mobs. For the first time since she'd known him, Karon worried about his safety. Ralph, a tall man, built like a football player, was not hurt in the disturbance, but he was hauled before a grand jury on the charge of injuring an unarmed, helpless onlooker. A photo was placed in evidence showing a big, burly policeman bent over, with his arms around the skinny chest of a young, long-haired news reporter. It looked like (and the caption read to this effect) a cop slamming a kid down on a concrete sidewalk. In fact, Ralph had been helping the man up. He was lucky that three witnesses had been present but still the incident shook Karon. She hadn't realized until then that there were forces an individual couldn't control. If Ralph was vulnerable, so was she. She didn't like it.

A few weeks later the nation got another jolt, another hint of an unrest and dissatisfaction growing beneath its veneer of the good life. A group of women's libbers reportedly threatened to burn their bras in protest of the annual Miss America contest at Atlantic City, and again on 7E the hooting began. Not one voice was raised in defense. The libbers were jeered. No one, not Karon, Joy nor any of the other women on the staff, supported what was happening. They saw the protesters as threats, as crazies with sick ideas, as people dissatisfied with their sex. In contrast they stood up and declared themselves proud to be female. Then they dismissed the libbers out of hand, turned around and placed odds on Miss Illinois' chances to win the crown. It would take another six years

18

for the real message of the 1968 Miss America protests to hit home for Karon and Joy. They would become part of the struggle and they would understand. Now they didn't care and saw no place for the movement in their lives.

Women's liberation simply gave Karon and Joy something new to talk about, and that's exactly what they were doing, with the rest of the staff, the afternoon Martha was brought to the floor. It was late September and the days were finally cooling from the intense summer heat. Martha was wheeled into admitting, a small, childlike brunette with chiseled features and pale green eyes that wandered aimlessly from one watching face to another. For a moment the staff forgot itself and stared at this strange young woman who looked so serene, holding a rag doll in her arms. Again the gulf between the sane and the bizarre asserted itself, almost paralyzing the staff with the immensity of the task they routinely undertook. Here was another one, pushed and pulled by unseen forces until she had to give in and release her hold on what was normal. Martha was from the maternity floor, where three days earlier she'd given birth to her first child, a seven-pound baby girl. According to the report Karon held in her hand, Martha, 22, had had a normal pregnancy and a routine delivery, but once back in her room she'd totally withdrawn from the world. She refused to see the baby and would not speak to her husband, doctor, or other patients.

When her mother asked if she wanted anything, Martha nodded yes and traced her finger along the white formica top of her bedside table to spell out the word KAT, her nickname for her favorite doll, one she'd had as a child. The next day Martha's mother brought the doll to the hospital and ever since the patient had refused to give it up. For the last two days, Martha had sat in her bed, gently rocking the doll and ignoring anyone who came to her. Her baby, still unnamed and never held in its mother's arms, lay sleeping less than 50 feet down the hall in the hospital nursery.

Psych patients have their own private ways of dealing with each other. Most often they are defensive and belligerent, painfully aware of their own weaknesses and determined to hit the soft spots in others. They snitch on each other, complain about each other's bad habits or antisocial behavior, and do their best to goad nervous, angry patients into tantrums. But at the same time, no group of people can be as protective and tolerant. This was the face the patients on 7E turned toward Martha. There were no jokes, no jibes or snickers. Rather, they treated the lonely young woman with deference and sympathy, as if they understood what had happened to her and were saddened by it. When Martha silently drifted into the OT (occupational therapy) room, rag doll in her arms, the men stood and awkwardly offered their seats, the women reached out smiling and touched her long shining hair with trembling fingers. When she moved noiselessly down the U-shaped hallway, orderlies stepped from her path and even the nurses deferred, watching in amazement as this strange angelic figure floated by.

Karon saw all this and was disturbed. The patient was becoming more introverted and was mentally disintegrating. The balance was all wrong, Karon told Joy over a Coke that night. The patient, because of the strange reactions she invoked in others, was determining procedure and defining her own treatment, which in this instance amounted to almost nothing. That night, Karon dreamt of Martha and the next morning woke up, knowing what she had to do.

At work, Karon checked first with the patient's doctor and got his approval for her plan. Then she bided her time. Dinner came and went, visiting hours were past, and finally the patients were coming together as they did automatically every evening. Some had dressed in pajamas already, others still wore their street clothes from the day. Only Martha wore the regulation hospital gown and the thin blue cotton robe issued routinely to all but psych patients. Most of them were in the dayroom, sitting around card tables playing gin rummy or pinochle or spread out on couches and chairs watching TV. Martha stood between the two groups, leaning one hip gently against the table tennis unit no one was using. She stared straight ahead toward the window, cradling KAT to her breast, looking as if she could have been standing alone on the moon. This was the quiet time, when not much usually happened, and at first no one paid any attention that evening when Karon walked into the room. The young charge nurse appeared casual and unconcerned as she slowly moved around the periphery, ending up as if by accident on the same side of the games table as Martha. By the time Karon pivoted to face the woman with the doll, every eye in the room had turned their way. It was a disquieting tableau: nurse and patient, so similar yet so different, two people standing on either side of sanity.

"I want you to put the doll down," Karon said. Her voice carried through the room, colliding with that of the TV announcer. There was no other sound.

Martha continued to look past her. "I want you to put the doll down." This time it was an order.

Karon had been cautious and deliberate. Now she moved quickly. Before anyone realized what she intended, Karon grabbed KAT from Martha's arms. She moved past the patient, trying to reach the doorway and the plastic garbage container next to it. Martha wheeled and screamed as the nurse dropped the doll into the trash. Suddenly all the patients were on their feet, yelling at Karon, cursing her. One lady spat in her direction and another made a grandiose obscene gesture, but no one moved. Through the din Karon called to Martha, who stood weeping and nervously pulling at the fabric of her robe just above the knees. Finally Karon stepped toward the patient and led her out the door and to her room. "Bitch! Bitch! Bitch!" the chant went up as Karon made her exit.

For two days the patients got back at the "Witch in White." They complained when they encountered her in the hall, threw food on the floor at dinner, or ignored her when she talked to them. At Wednesday night's weekly family living discussion, they were waiting to crucify her. For 30 minutes Karon sat through accusations and tirades, listening to the patients tell how terrible and unfair she was. She'd walked into the meeting nervous and unsure of herself, but as her turn to talk approached she grew more resolute.

"I understand how you all feel about me," she began. "I know you think I did a horrible thing, but you forget why I'm here. I'm supposed to help you, if you can believe that. I'm not here to win any popularity contests. It's nice if you like me, if you like all of us, but that's not what matters. It's my job to help you get better. That's what counts, not that you agree with me, but that you get better. I treat you with what you need—not with what you think you need."

The next week Martha was discharged. She could have left the unit in the early afternoon but she waited until the second shift started. Her husband walked down the hall with her, past the silent, watchful eyes of the other patients. When they reached the nurses' station, just before they stepped through the locked steel door, Martha hesitated and turned toward Karon. She stared at her a moment, this time with eyes that were steady, and stretched out her hand.

"Thank you," she said. "I never could have done it myself. I couldn't put it down."

This incident did much to cement the relationship between Joy and Karon. Joy was the only one on the floor to defend the younger nurse, the only one who seemed to understand what she'd done and why. In her seven years of caring for the sick, Joy had seen too many instances of nurses being buddies and friends to patients. She'd seen them hide behind rules, back off from confrontations, and retreat to their stations, keeping their jobs secure but watching their resolve disintegrate. "We're all hesitant," she told Gordon. "Me as much as the rest. They teach us that in school, then make sure we never forget. But Karon's not afraid."

Less than a week later, Joy learned she was pregnant. Suddenly her world, which had briefly begun opening up, closed in. She was caught between her deep personal joy at having a child and the realization of how much this happiness would cost. Hospital rules demanded she quit at the end of the fourth month, because just recently a pregnant aide had been kicked in the stomach by a patient. The new policy meant spending the worst part of winter at home, with no extra money coming in and two small children as her only companions.

Worse, Gordon would accuse her of the unthinkable. He'd done it once already, with the second child, and there was no reason to think it wouldn't happen again. Nor would his jealousy abate—that she knew. Gordon was like an innocent, a gentle man gone mad with alcohol. Sober, he wouldn't raise his voice, much less his hand, but after only a few beers he changed radically. In the back of her mind Joy kept one thought, one fear, tightly under control: what if he used the gun? Every policeman had one, 24 hours a day, in the holster or somewhere in the house. Gordon kept his on the top shelf of their bedroom closet.

Overwhelmed, Joy turned to Karon, confiding her fears to her after work. To Karon, still fresh from her victory with Martha, the solution was simple. Joy had to stand up for herself, request a work extension from the hospital, tell Gordon to go to hell, stop letting others push her around. But Joy couldn't. The image of authority was too powerful for her to fight, her own sense of shyness and fear of attention too strong to combat. She was convinced that some people are born with the ability to get away with things and others are not. If she'd been as demanding with Gordon as Karon was with Ralph, she'd be in even worse straits; if she'd stood up to Martha as Karon had, the patient probably would have become catatonic and the family would have sued her. No, for Joy the only answer was to yield, to offer the least resistance to the battering winds of her life.

It was a lively time on 7E. They had a 16-year-old pregnant girl, admitted as the basis for obtaining a legal abortion. For a few days they had a 39-year-old convicted murderer, released on parole after spending twenty years in jail for beating a young boy to death

23

with a chair. The patient refused to bathe or change his clothing and spent all his time in the bathroom where he stood with his feet in the air, his shoulders resting on the toilet bowl rim, and his head inside the bowl, trying to cleanse himself.

Soon afterward, a depressed multiple sclerosis victim, a young executive in his mid-30s, was sent up for observation. He had fantasies of raping women and had reportedly tried to attack one nurse on the medical floor. Karon felt sorry for him and contrary to normal procedure went into his room alone one afternoon to talk. The man was bedridden and her guard was down. Unthinking she turned around to adjust the window blinds and in the next instant was almost whipped off balance by the cane he'd snagged around her ankle. It took two orderlies, big men themselves, to subdue the rage of the patient.

A week later, a local politician's mother was admitted to the floor with an unspecified nervous condition. The grand old lady, heir to a large fortune, got more attention than any patient ever had on the unit. Her psychiatrist came by every morning, and then her daughter-in-law appeared in the afternoon.

"Mrs. Harry Harrison here!" she called out each time she sailed past the nurses' station, her right arm raised in a salute, until the staff couldn't take it anymore.

"Miss Karon White here!" boomed a friendly retort one Friday, to the delight of the staff and to the displeasure of Mrs. H.

By the second week of the old woman's stay it had become obvious that the 62-year-old patient had a crush on her 33-year-old doctor. She walked him to the door after each visit, her delicate hand holding gently to his arm. To discourage her, because it was interfering with her treatment, the doctor asked Karon to pretend to be his girlfriend.

"I'll walk up to you at the nurses' station after I see her and ask you for a date for that night," he explained. "She'll hear me, then see how ridiculous her ideas are."

That night Karon went home with a large black and blue welt on her left shin where the politician's mother had kicked her.

24

Another patient, a middle-aged woman, refused to talk intelligently to any of the staff. Most of the time, she rambled on, repeating her own nonsense phrase: "Either or, neither nor. Maybe, maybe not."

She was walking down the hall one afternoon reciting her chant when she came up to Karon. "Dime," the patient said, indicating that she wanted to make a phone call.

Karon looked at the woman a moment, then quietly said, "Either or, neither nor. Maybe, maybe not."

"Are you nuts?" asked the woman.

"No," said Karon. "Are you?"

The patient was too taken aback to answer. But from that day on she communicated normally with everyone on the floor.

On Thanksgiving, the day Joy learned that a doctor she had once worked with had shot and killed his wife and himself, Alex was brought to the floor. He was a short, thin man with a square, pockmarked face and thinning brown hair, a former machine shop foreman who was convinced J. Edgar Hoover was after him. When he talked at all, Alex rambled on about conspiracies and double agents. He paced constantly, looking over his shoulder for spies. From the first night Joy checked his room he'd been suspicious of her, convinced she was taking down notes about him. Twice he refused to take his medication from her and once he overturned the table where she'd placed his dinner tray.

One night, Alex paced steadily in the hallway near the nurses' station, glowering at Karon and Barbara, the only staff on duty. The orderly had gone for coffee and the two women waited. They weren't so much afraid as cautious. If they stayed still, Alex might go away on his own. But if they moved, if a call button lit up, he could become dangerous. The last time he'd been put in restraints, it had taken five adults, three of them men, to subdue him. Alex knew what power he had and he flexed it, stepping silently in the small square section of hallway. But they had power over him, these two, the power of his own fear. Slowly, smoothly, Barbara reached toward the button that activated the intercom system. Just as Alex reached the end of his stride and turned to retrace his steps, her voice rang between the walls. "Alex, this is J. Edgar Hoover speaking. Go to bed. I repeat—go to bed." It worked. "You know, that's not good treatment," Karon said to the other nurse. "But it sure worked—it saved our necks."

Another day, when Alex was in restraints under doctor's orders, he bounced and wiggled enough to maneuver his bed four feet across the room, making enough noise to alert the unit that something was up. Together Joy and Karon went to check on him. Karon kicked the door and waited thirty seconds, all the time it took for a heavy wooden drawer, pulled from the night table stand, to slam into the door jamb, at the height her head would have been had she walked immediately into the room.

"It is physically impossible for any patient in restraints to have done that," the psychiatrist responded when Karon reported the incident. Despite her argument, the doctor refused to have his patient transferred to an institution for the more violent. Alex was to spend his Christmas on 7E.

Despite all the good will of friends and family, despite the cookies from the ladies' clubs, the carols from the local high school groups, and the cheap candy in the tacky plastic bags one psychiatrist brought in every year as his big treat, Christmas is a bad time in the hospital. All hope seems to evaporate that one day and all the loneliness in the world comes here to roost. The more promising patients go home on two- or three-day passes, making the holidays better for them but worse for those who must remain. Karon had worked one other Christmas and made the mistake that time of trying to fight the overwhelming mood. This time she kept a low profile. She was the only nurse on duty after seven; two aides and an orderly were assigned to her shift but the latter hadn't appeared. With special permission, visitors had been allowed on the ward all day and they had helped with a family-style staff and patient dinner and with the clean-up. By the time family and friends left, the unit was quiet. Most of the patients were tired and had gone to their rooms, another special privilege given that one evening. Only a few watched TV in the OT room. Karon sat at the nurses' station, flipping through a report. At one point, the phone rang and Joy and her children shouted "Merry Christmas" across the wires. Then came her parents and brothers and later Ralph called from work to say hello. Finally it was time for rounds. Both aides were off the floor so Karon went herself.

Alex wasn't in his bed. Karon checked the dayroom and the OT room. Empty. She knew the conference and laundry rooms were locked. That left the kitchen. But he wasn't there either.

On her guard now Karon hurried through the quiet hall back to the station, her greatest fear that Alex had somehow escaped with the departing guests. It had happened once before, not here, when a man had gotten out of a locked ward and stolen a car to go home and kill his father. The patient might have succeeded, too, if it hadn't been a police car he'd taken. Karon was thinking of this other man now, debating whether to call security or keep looking herself, when she saw Alex standing at the exit door. He had his coat on. Karon stopped in the hallway, her back toward the wall, and gambled that this time, as he had done before, Alex would respond to a firm, direct order.

"Go to your room," Karon directed. Alex hunched his shoulders and studied the floor for a moment. Then he turned slowly around in a complete circle, humming quietly. Karon didn't budge. "Go to your room for room check," she insisted once more. Alex stopped moving. He looked intently at Karon, then lowered his head, turned from the door, and began walking back into the ward, wiggling out of his coat as he proceeded. By the time Alex was even with Karon he had one arm free, dangling inside the long brown overcoat. He hunched his shoulders as if to slip his other arm loose but instead spun on his heels, whipped his body around and slapped the full force of the free hand across Karon's face, knocking her off balance. With the coat hanging clumsily from his left shoulder, Alex lunged at the nurse and grasped her throat. He pulled her forward, away from the wall, trying to kick her feet out from under her.

Alex was no fool; he knew exactly how many people stood between him and the outside. All he had to do to get out was grab the keys from Karon's pocket and keep her from reaching the phone that sat idly only ten feet away. She would call Hoover and in minutes they'd be all over him. He had to stop her. He could feel the sweat on his forehead, could feel the viselike strength of his arms squeezing his hands tighter.

Alex was fighting for freedom and he fought hard, but he hadn't calculated how hard someone else might fight for life. With her elbows and feet, Karon pummeled him. The heel of his left foot slid down her leg, tearing her white nylon stocking as she grabbed his hair in the only place it was thick, down around the neck. Then suddenly, loudly, she began to kick the wall, and finally, with one slip of Alex's hand, Karon was able to call out. In seconds, the agents were there, disguised as patients. They pulled Alex down and sat on him until Karon stopped shaking.

Alex spent Christmas night in restraints. Karon spent it trying to convince Ralph and her parents that the entire incident was nothing to get excited about. She wouldn't admit to anyone how scared she had been.

chapter two

*B*y September, 1969, Karon White had a flashy engagement ring to show off and Joy Catterson had a new baby to brag about. The two had been separated since the first of the year when Joy quit the hospital on maternity leave, but almost effortlessly they picked up where their friendship had left off. After nine months at home, nine months away from work—five of them with a colicky baby and one with summer pneumonia—Joy was delighted to be on the job again. Despite her boredom a year earlier, the first day back in psych had been pure heaven, the first night out with Karon and the rest of the small staff had been so refreshing Joy could almost taste the sweetness of it in the air.

Since January her uniforms had hung in the back of her closet, her white shoes had sat on the floor while she waited for the baby. The first few months had been awful for Joy. At four months, she barely showed, had no problems bending or moving around, but was forced to go on leave because of hospital policy. At home Joy virtually bounced off the walls, her tremendous energy propelling her about without purpose. The only really necessary task was to shovel snow, the one job she wouldn't do. Gordon needed the exercise more, she reasoned. So Joy cleaned closets, rearranged kitchen cabinets, changed draperies, and, weather permitting, bundled her two little ones off to a nearby shopping center for nothing more than looking around. Joy refused to buy herself anything while she was pregnant; she hated herself fat and thought only of later and a slim body.

But when the baby's time came, Joy was ready. She loved children, felt completed and whole in the process of giving birth, delighted in the freshness and simplicity of the infant. Joy was proud to have children, proud of them as independent souls and of herself in the capacity of mother. But although in one sense children were enough for her, in another sense she didn't fully understand, she wanted more. Joy needed her job, her identity as RN, her responsibilities in another place outside the home, responsibilities that had nothing to do with being a wife or a parent. Now back at work, even if just two days a week, she felt a sense of equilibrium in her life. Joy was happy.

"How has everything been up here?" she asked Karon the first time the two ended up together in the medication room.

"Okay. Like always."

The words were music to Joy. She wasn't looking for any changes. She was simply hungry for the job she'd missed. "It sure is nice to be back," she said. To herself she thought, too, that it was nice to have Karon still in charge.

"You must be doing a good job," Joy remarked later over pizza at their favorite restaurant.

"It's okay," Karon replied, but she smiled. She was doing a damn good job and she loved it. She was pleased too that Joy had returned. Karon genuinely enjoyed working in the psych ward and Joy was the only other nurse she knew who shared the feeling with her. The others seemed tentative about being behind the locked doors. They always asked to be transferred, and couldn't understand why anyone like Karon would want to stay there on a long-term basis. All except Joy. She understood. The still fledgling team was back together. They'd have their hands full too.

Twice that fall Karon would have to put her staff on suicide watch. Patients who threatened, mentioned, or acted as if they might try suicide could not be left alone. Twenty-four hours a day, a guardian angel hung on their shoulders, because they could not be trusted on their own for any length of time. The watch put a pall on the entire unit, for although new patients might not catch on to the situation, the old-timers and repeaters quickly picked up the pattern and soon word was out. A relaxed atmosphere turned rigid; a tense one became almost unbearable. The potentially suicidal patient and his or her angel suddenly were center stage, pirouetting in a bizarre death dance made more eerie because no one knew whether to take it seriously or not. Usually the other patients acted like spectators at a bullfight or the Indy 500, divided into those who wanted to see a little blood and those who, once they realized what could possibly happen, also realized that they'd rather not be in the stands. Unfortunately, they had no choice, because the stands were locked and marked No Exit.

One potential suicide was a woman who was having an affair with a man who was both her brother and an ordained priest. The other problem patient was Sandra, a young woman who had lost her husband in a car crash. Sandra seemed to suffer from a combination of ills, and she hallucinated imaginary friends and enemies alike. During the day Sandra often walked the halls muttering satanic curses, directing them at the staff and at other patients. Every night Sandra changed into a white negligee, then lay on her bed with her feet up in imaginary stirrups. The entire floor heard her groan and scream as she delivered her pretend baby. When a patient would ask Sandra about the newborn the next day she'd say, "screw you," then wander off grabbing tufts of her hair and pulling them up in an attempt to make herself taller.

Although Sandra accepted her medication, she resisted any other attempts on the part of the staff to help her. She would not talk to her one-to-one, and she sat tight-lipped during the current events classes Karon insisted she attend. To Karon, Sandra was just another patient, perhaps a little more unsettling because she was so young and had already had more than her share of bad luck. But for Sandra, the tall, clipped charge nurse became a symbol to hate and destroy. She accused Karon of having an affair with her father and once tore the nurse's wig from her head. "Phony, phony," Sandra said. "I'm going to tell the doctor you're a phony."

Later Sandra threatened suicide.

"I'm going to kill myself on your shift, so you'll get fired," she told Karon one evening during dinner. Thirty-three sets of ears heard it and the watch was on.

"I know she's bluffing," Karon told Joy. "She is *not* suicidal, she's not the type, but I can't take any chances."

In two-hour shifts, the staff babysat for Sandra. One day went by, then two and three. Each evening a different nurse had to sit through Sandra's deliveries, which grew succeedingly more grotesque and elaborate and more pathetic. On the fourth day of the mental tug of war, nerves were taut and frayed all around. Karon, the angel for the rest of the evening, had followed Sandra from the OT room to the dayroom, down the hall to the laundry room, and up the hall to the kitchen.

"All this high-priced attention, I can hardly stand it." Sandra baited the nurse, but got no response.

"I'm going to take a bath and you can't come in," she taunted.

"That's okay," Karon finally replied. "I'll know what you're doing behind the door anyway."

"Ooh, nasty. You really think you're smart, White. But I'll fix you. I'll drown myself. I'll do it on your shift."

Karon brought a chair from a patient's room and set it down in the hall next to the bathroom door. As she sat there, listening to the running water inside, she prayed and wondered. Sandra needed to cry, to make that one wild primordial scream at the moon that we all sometimes need to make and then she needed to reach out for a friend. And Karon suspected that Sandra realized this and for that reason would not kill herself, because the drive behind her anger was an intense desire for life and living. Still, once begun, the scenario must be played out, hopefully to the right ending.

"What time will the body be ready?" Karon asked through the door.

"What time is it now?"

"Four-twenty."

"Okay. I'll be ready at five."

"Do you have a preference for a funeral director?"

32

"Yes. My cousin."

"What's his name?"

"Joe Blow, 648-9218."

The voice had changed. It was tired now. The plot had grown stale, the principal actor bored with the role. When Karon heard the water draining from the tub and saw flashes of white towel through the partially open door she silently moved the chair back across the hall to where she'd gotten it and stood quietly inspecting a piece of the wall ten feet from the bathroom when Sandra finally emerged. The next day, Karon reported the incident in detail to the patient's doctor and with his permission ended the watch. Within two weeks the nightly deliveries began to taper off and eventually Sandra went home. Like many patients, she was not completely cured, but at least she'd reached a level where she could function normally within her own world.

Three weeks before Christmas Angie arrived. She was young, only 24, but would prove one of the most difficult patients admitted to 7E. Angie was brought in at 2:00 A.M. after the police found her wandering inside the first floor lobby of the main post office. She was looking for her boyfriend, she explained. He worked there and he had promised to marry her and now she couldn't find him. For thirty minutes Angie had run up and down the marble floor beating on the closed windows that lined the inside wall of the lobby, screaming her boyfriend's name. She'd been brought screaming to the psych ward and she had screamed throughout the night.

The next day Angie's mother, a nervous little woman with an Eastern European accent, told the resident psychiatrist that Angie didn't really have a boyfriend. The young man was one her daughter had dated four or five times. Angie was upset, her mother said, because all her friends were getting married. Last year alone, Angie had been invited to seven wedding showers and seven weddings. Each time she'd come home crying, clutching tiny pink paper baskets and white fold-out paper bells. At the last wedding Angie had caught the bride's bouquet, which she'd wrapped in plastic and stuck in the freezer. Since then, she'd been clipping out pictures of wedding dresses and "acting strange."

During the day shift, Angie underwent electroshock treatment, prescribed by her doctor. Three times a week she was strapped to a bed with an IV injection of sodium amytal hooked to her right arm, an injection of anectine and atropine flowing through her veins, and a rubber safety device in her mouth, to keep her from biting her tongue. Relaxed and unconscious, Angie was ready for the electrodes to be attached to her head. Then, while she lay immersed in another world, the electricity was turned on. It coursed from the generator, through the wires, into the electrode connectors, and finally into the young woman's brain and from there into her body. The shock was eerie to watch, like witnessing Dr. Frankenstein jolt his monster into action. For a few seconds (which seemed longer) the patient stiffened as if dead, with limbs and muscles tensed to the extreme. Then it was all over and the doctors and nurses unhooked their equipment and wheeled it off to an unmarked room. The patient, still unconscious, was left alone with an orderly or aide.

Angie was fantasizing, almost hallucinating, unable to distinguish between reality and the imaginary world she had created, one focused on an imaginary boyfriend figure. It was hoped that shock treatments, which interrupt ongoing thought patterns, would help her break through the fantasy and deal with the reality at hand. Eventually, the therapy would succeed, but in the interim, the regimen produced confusion and memory loss in the young woman's mind. The Angie whom Karon and the afternoon shift dealt with was an angry, distraught woman caught in a web of almost hopeless temporary confusion brought on by the treatments. She talked about make-believe wedding plans but suddenly found herself unable to remember her home phone number or her mother's first name. Once Angie tried to tell another patient where she'd been born and when she couldn't come up with the name of the city, she went berserk, screaming up and down the halls that the nurses were trying to steal her mind.

34

Angie was afraid, and her fear was contagious. Yet all the staff could do was sympathize and try as gently as possible to help her.

"Don't let yourself get aggravated with her," Karon told the staff at its weekly meeting. "She needs extra consideration and we have to give it to her. As you know, what she is going through isn't very pleasant. In fact, I doubt if any of you would want those electrodes on your head. So I don't want to hear any reports of anyone on this shift being short with her."

Then Karon went back to the station to talk to the supervisor, asking why patients were not hooked up to an electrocardiograph machine while the shock treatments were administered. The procedure is not time-consuming, Karon pointed out, is standard at other hospitals, and could prove crucial in monitering the patient's condition should the treatment affect the heart. Shortly after Christmas, Angie finally left the hospital, a sad, subdued woman returning to an empty life. But Karon never got an official response to her query. Instead, word came up that the nursing director didn't think it right for nurses to question hospital procedures.

The new year kicked off with Karon questioning another hospital rule. This time she received an answer. The day before, Joy had been one of six nurses needed to subdue a violent patient. The patient was strong and the women had to struggle with flailing arms and legs. Joy, the smallest, was kneeling on the foot of the bed when the patient's legs were finally quieted. Quickly but carefully Joy straddled the almost stilled body, jockeying for position so she could administer a tranquilizing shot of Thorazine. She was nearly face to face with the patient when an arm shot up from nowhere and grabbed her crotch. Red-faced and startled, Joy tumbled off to the side.

Why, Karon asked her supervisor, did the hospital insist on nurses wearing dress uniforms? Pants would be more practical, as well as more modest. They would not detract from the RN's image and would even make much of the nurse's job easier. Could her staff have permission to wear pants? The reply was short: No.

(Eventually, the hospital administrators did allow nurses to dress in pants, stating in the official announcement. however. that they hoped "our nurses would stay ladies and not wear them.")

Then one Monday morning, Karon walked into the psych ward to learn that over the weekend a student nurse had been badly injured when she'd gone in, alone, to check on a patient in restraints. State law dictates that a locked-door ward have at least one registered nurse and one orderly on duty at all times. Hospital rules go further and say that when a patient is in restraints, no RN, LPN, student nurse, or doctor should enter the room without additional personnel for personal protection. The student had gone in, and as she bent over to check the waist restraint, the patient, with only one arm secured, grabbed the blood pressure machine and began beating the student nurse on the head. The girl ended up in the ER for treatment and was given an official reprimand. The next day she was tranferred out of psych.

"Why did you do that?" Karon asked her.

The student claimed she had no choice. She had been told to check on the patient and she had to do it. If there'd been an orderly on duty, she would have taken him along, but none worked that particular shift.

Between the Sandras and the Angies, between the crotch-grabbers and the attackers, life went on rather routinely on 7E. As the charge nurse, Karon was always busy. Once a week she met with her staff to discuss problems and procedure; once a month she attended an in-service meeting where she and other specialty nurses took turns giving presentations about their areas of expertise, a task not included in Karon's job description but one she had to take on for her supervisor. On some Saturdays the charge nurse also sat in on the discharge meetings held for patients and families. And regularly Karon scheduled current events classes, makeup demonstrations, even cake decorating sessions. All this was in addition to the daily floor routines of supervising meals, assigning patient care to the floor nurses, monitoring medications, reviewing patient charts, ordering drugs, conferring with doctors, and trying to keep relatives up to date on patient progress.

For the most part, the ward functioned smoothly, The second shift worked well together and seemed to enjoy doing that little extra measure for their charges. Weather permitting, Joy or another floor nurse took selected patients on walks through the neighborhood or to a local health club for an hour's swimming. Occasionally, a spontaneous dance was thrown together when Karon, Joy, and anyone else on duty two-stepped with patients and urged wallflowers to seek out partners. There was time for a few laughs, too, like the evening Joy and an orderly fell into the tub together trying to get an obese patient up and on his feet after a bath.

And always there were surprises. "I don't know what to order," a patient complained one afternoon as he perused the dinner menu. "I don't like any of this stuff." "So ask for a steak instead," Karon said facetiously. When the dinner trays arrived, there were 29 orders of turkey and perch and one T-bone steak. "Steak?" Karon inquired in a call to the kitchen. "Oh sure, we keep that stuff around in case someone asks; we even got lobster. Just keep it quiet." From then on, however, the psych ward would send an occasional order for one of the more exotic dishes, a good idea especially on weekends when some patients were out on pass and there was no one but the nurses to eat the uncamcelled dinners.

*   *   *   *   *

Unlike the staff on medical/surgery floors, the nurses on 7E rarely came in contact with regular physicians. If psych patients became physically ill, they were either transferred out of the unit or one of the hospital residents came up for consultation. Otherwise, only staff and private duty psychiatrists came to the floor. Technically, the psychiatrists were supposed to visit the patients three times a week, usually during the morning, but many did not. The nurses ran the floor; they did whatever counseling was done; they talked to family members; they observed patient behavior and made recommendations for changes in treatment; they administered the prescribed drugs and charted reactions for the doctors to read about later.

When an MD appeared on the floor, most of the nurses were deferential. They'd been taught in school to get out of the way, to step back or stand up, almost to salute, and no one doubted for a second that such behavior was necessary for the proper functioning of the institution. Even Karon, the most outspoken nurse on the floor, deferred, at least initially. She admired and respected all the doctors at first, then became more discriminating. The other nurses were probably more awed by the psychiatrists than she was, but none of them doubted—not for a moment—the power the doctors wielded. A doctor could have a nurse fired or transferred simply on his—for most of them were men—word. A doctor could write an order to cover a mistake and no one would question it. A doctor could do almost anything he wanted—and this could mean he did much or did little for a particular patient—and rarely have to answer for it.

One psychiatrist on the floor, for example, was famous for hanging up the phone whenever relatives called to ask about a patient. He thought it was a big joke. "If the patient is important enough to them, they'll call back," he'd always say, laughing. Another one had a theory that schizophrenics shouldn't be cured "because then they become murderers," so he never did much to help any schizos under his care. Often the phone would ring in late afternoon, a doctor calling to ask a specific nurse—they all had certain staff members they trusted more than others—to check on a patient and to talk to the person for a while because "I don't have time today."

For the most part, the hospital consisted of two different worlds of authority and sex floating past each other, intermingling at times, but generally functioning in separate spheres. The men were always addressed with authority; they were "Doctor" on day one and "Doctor" thirty years later. The women, on the other hand, were treated like girls next door; they were never "Nurse," but plain old Barbara or Mary or sometimes "Doll" or "Honey." The men gave the orders; the women filled them. Even when the nurses were obviously running the show, ostensibly they weren't.

38

The men were free agents; the women were hospital employees. The men could not function without the women, yet it was the women who were put in the position of being thankful for their jobs. In many respects, the status quo of the hospital reflected that of the rest of the world at the time, and no one on 7E questioned it.

At least on the psych ward there were no doctor/nurse affairs going on. In fact, there were probably fewer such relationships in the entire hospital than the general public assumed. No one had time for it, for one thing, and few people were really interested, perhaps because they dealt with each other in the realistic world of medicine, not in the glamorous hospital life the public saw on television. There were no Dr. Kildares at General Community and only a rare Ben Casey. But there were plenty of doctors who yelled and cursed, had bad breath, were overweight and irritable, some who were pompous, some who were rude, a few who thought it hysterical to make snide remarks about nurses' breasts and jokes about female genitals. A favorite trick, in fact, was to have the hospital operator page "Dr. Hyman Clitoris."

The majority, though, were men doing a job, men whose own wives or girlfriends came first in their lives. The same with the nursing staff. For every hot-lipped, bed-hopping siren, there were a hundred nurses who were either too old to care or too in love with someone else to be interested. Sure, there were cases of true love forming across the lines, as well as examples of barter in which youth and good looks traded off with prestige and money, no questions asked, but these were exceptions. In truth, the two camps rarely had much to do with each other; the doctors, especially, couldn't be bothered with the nursing staff.

Some of the doctors respected the nurses' professional status; some did not. One psychiatrist, for example, tried to recruit nurses to work as domestics at his house on their days off. "Don't worry, I'll pay," he'd assure them. "The work is light anyway. You just get the orders from my wife. She does one room at a time, one room a day." The nurses didn't like him, mainly because he was serious. He didn't tease them like the other MDs; he used them to bolster his own ego and to flaunt his own greater status and money. Behind his back they called him "Doctor Bill" because of his preoccupation with the trappings of wealth "Doctor Bill phoned Chez Paul today for a dinner reservation, using our phone, just so we'd know he's going there," was a familiar report. Or, "Don't call Doctor Bill at home this evening—he's out on the other acre again."

Another doctor, an internist, had no respect for anything that went on up on the psych ward and no use for anyone affiliated with it, psychiatrists or nurses. "It's all a bunch of mumbo jumbo," he'd say, even though his twin brother was a psychiatrist. Whenever a surgical patient needed counseling and a psych nurse came down, he'd complain and curse about interference. When a psych patient became ill and he was sent up to do a physical exam, he came in grumbling.

One afternoon the nurses were ready for him. The doctor had finished examining a middle-aged man who had been complaining of chest pains and hot flashes when Karon, Joy, and Sheila, the three on duty, went into action. They sent the aide off the floor on an errand; they sent the orderly to the pharmacy to check on a drug order. Karon hid in the laundry room and Joy and Sheila went out the locked door to the service elevator to use the phone. When the doctor emerged from the patient's room the hall was empty except for two old neurotic ladies walking and babbling past him. The nurses' station was deserted. The physician looked around, uneasily. Televisions and voices groaned in the background.

"Anybody here? I have to leave a report." The doctor's words died in the silence surrounding the station. He was bent over the counter, writing a note, when the phone rang.

"I'm going to kill myself," the voice, a female voice, screamed.

"Wait. Who is this—stop—where are you?"

"I'm here. I'm going to kill myself."

"No, wait. Please, I'll get a nurse."

40

But the line went dead.

"Nurse! Nurse!" The doctor began yelling. In two steps he was out in the hall, running. "Nurse! Nurse!"

Eventually, even the doctor admitted it was a good joke. He never criticized the psych nurses again.

Outside the wards, the doctors did not usually associate with other staff members, except for a few rare parties. Even in the cafeteria, the staff was segregated, as it was in the lounges scattered throughout the hospital. The medical staff members all spoke the same language but seemed to do so in different dialects, and so talked very little, unless something out of the ordinary was going on, like the time the Arab intern was on duty. He either didn't know about the unspoken rules or else didn't care, because he associated freely with everyone. He'd ask the nurses questions about their lives and answer questions about his country. But he was most popular for his palm-reading talents.

It was late in the afternoon when Dr. Samedi, a young, good-natured man, came to the psych ward. He was curious, he said, about the setup and asked for a tour. An hour later, he was in the floor lounge reading palms.

"You are the oldest girl in your family."

Karon nodded. She thought palm reading was ridiculous and was going to prove it. Dr. Samedi was new at General Community; he'd never been on her floor before and they had never met. She waited for him to say something ludicrous.

"You have three younger brothers."

Karon nodded again.

"Your grandfather had been a wealthy man, but he lost his money—I am not sure how."

Karon and Joy looked at each other. No one knew about that except them.

"You will be married next year."

"Yes" was all Karon could manage, but she flushed, thinking of her engagement ring hidden in her pocket. She hadn't wanted to give him any clues.

"You will go someplace across an ocean, but you are not going to Europe."

Karon and Ralph had talked about a honeymoon in Hawaii.

"You yourself are not going to have children. But I still see a girl in your future. It is not clear who she is."

By this point Joy had her sleeves rolled up and had squeezed in behind Karon. This guy is good, she thought. There was a lot she wanted to know about her future and this seemed as good a way of finding out as any. The other nurses, who didn't know about Ralph's previous marriage because Karon had been embarrassed to tell them, whispered that most of it had been amazing— lucky guesses—but the last statement was a real stab in the dark, a fancy hedge.

"Well, Dr. Samedi, if you don't make it as an intern, you can always get a job with the circus."

It was a stupid joke and Karon regretted saying it immediately. Dr. Samedi looked at her and nodded, then he reached for Joy's hand, just as his buzzer sounded.

"Sorry," he shrugged. "Perhaps another day." He gave them a polite half bow before walking toward the locked door. Except there were no other days. Dr. Samedi transferred out of the hospital shortly afterward, leaving Karon with her questions of how and Joy with her guesses of her own tomorrows.

The two women didn't talk too much those days about their changing roles in relation to their jobs. They talked about the things that happened—negative, sometimes subtly degrading events—but not about what it all meant. Perhaps it was too early for them to see a pattern or perhaps they were too busy with their own lives to sit around and analyze. Joy was pregnant again, and most of Karon's free time went toward wedding preparations. Because they took on the hospital one day at a time, isolating events, not linking them, they thought Dr. Surrella's treatment of Bernadette Rommel, one of their fellow nurses, meant he was a bastard. That's all. They saw little else in it, not enough to cause them to rally round the flag, something they didn't know how to

42

do anyway. They certainly saw no link yet between what was happening to them and what women in the outside world were beginning to grumble about.

Dr. Surrela had a teenaged patient on the floor and had asked Bernadette to be the boy's one-to-one, with the promise of some possible ouside work later. Bernadette, whose brother had been in the same medical school class as Dr. Surrela, agreed and spent much energy and time with the patient. When the boy was released, he remained under Dr. Surrela's care and Bernadette was hired to counsel both him and his parents at the psychiatrist's office. "He's going to pay me twenty dollars an hour," Bernadette told the other nurses, for whom such a fee was unheard of. Ten visits later Bernadette had not been paid. When she complained, Surrela handed her a check for $40. "He told me that I didn't understand, that I was only a nurse and that the corporation got 40 percent and then the psychologist had to be paid for supervising me and that I only got what was left—three dollars an hour." It was another late-night pizza conference and Bernadette, confused and humiliated, sat shaking and almost in tears. Her anger spread to her friends, Karon, Joy, and Sheila, but they could only sit helpless in their fury.

"Damn!" Karon said.

"Yeah. Damn and then what?" Joy posed it as a question, but she knew she'd get no answer.

The nurses did the only thing they could do, tell and retell the story until they were sick of hearing it and had to go home.

The following week Karon received word that Dr. Surrela was wanted for a consultation with a depressed surgical patient on a medical floor. She phoned his office to tell him about the case. She spoke directly to Surrela and left the necessary information with him. One week later, after the doctor had been asked repeatedly for his report on the patient, Karon was called in to her supervisor's office.

"Dr. Surrela wants to know what this is all about. He claims he could not possibly have known he was supposed to see this patient because he never heard of the gentleman. He assumes that if you gave the information to anyone, it was to his secretary, who must have misplaced it or forgotten about it."

"If I talked to his secretary, then I don't know the difference between a man's voice and woman's voice." Karon was firm. "I talked to the doctor."

The incident was never mentioned again. When Karon tried to discuss it with Surrela, he was busy. Within a month the entire matter had escaped his mind, but she remembered it.

As part of their jobs, the nurses monitored patient symptoms and actions to determine if prescribed procedures or treatments should be altered. Sometimes they misread the signs. Once they were convinced a psych patient was undergoing an acute appendicitis attack. But when the attending physician came up to investigate, he found the woman sitting up in bed smiling, her makeup in place, and a flimsy negligee covering her body. The patient's pain had mysteriously disappeared. More times than not, however, the nurses' judgements were on target and it hurt to see their advice shunned.

"He must be in restraints for the ambulance ride," Karon argued about a patient being transferred to another hospital. The doctor disagreed and refused to issue the order. That afternoon, while the patient was being transported, he attacked the attendant and, with his fists, broke the window in the back of the ambulance.

"A fool could see this man is deathly ill," Joy argued in another instance. "He is bloated, jaundiced, incredibly weak. It's inhuman to get him out of bed." But orders were orders. The patient had been admitted to one of the medical floors, then was sent up to the psych ward because "his illness is all in his head." He was to be walked three times a day. The nurses were to force him up if they had to. "But he has three-plus edema," Joy explained to the man's doctor over the phone. "He literally has death written all over him. His symptoms are abnormal. Please, at least, have an intern and a neurologist sent up to examine him." She was told there was nothing wrong, either with the patient or with the diagnosis. For two weeks Joy agonized over the patient and then one afternoon when she couldn't tolerate the situation any longer, she simply let the man lie in bed during his exercise period. Two days later he died. Of cancer. Joy went home disheartened from thinking of the pain that had been imposed on the man.

The nurses' lack of official authority extended even beyond patient treatment. If they observed any wrongdoing, their lips were sealed. When a patient got loose from restraints one night on the graveyard shift (11 to seven) and beat up another patient, sending him to the ER with a concussion, the nurses had to mouth the official line. The injured patient had simply fallen out of bed. When an overdose patient was erroneously sent to the psych ward because the person who admitted her didn't believe the overdose story, despite the empty pill bottle her distraught husband brought in, and the patient died, the nurses could say nothing. In fact, in that incident, Karon had mentioned specific symptoms in her notes: the patient has rales, is spitting up, and is losing consciousness. The doctor she summoned to check the woman disputed all the symptoms the nurse had observed and made his own contradicting notes on the chart—which mysteriously disappeared during the night.

The nurse, it was becoming clear, was an adjunct and little else. She had to be there; rather, her RN license did, because the law required it. The message came loud and clear to Karon when she reported one nurse for being on drugs. "So what? A lot of nurses take drugs, that's what I was told," Karon told Joy over coffee. "They really don't care, do they? I report this nurse and I can't do anything else and they're going to do nothing about it." Another time Karon reported a nurse for using Valium and was told it was none of her business. ("It is my business, it's happening on my floor!" she screamed at Ralph.)

Once Joy had worked with an older nurse who'd recently been hired after many years out of the profession. The woman asked to be assigned to medications, meaning she would be responsible for distributing drugs to the patients on the floor. One day Joy watched the woman take a full syringe of a narcotic drug into a bathroom and emerge with an empty syringe and blood running down her arm. The supervisor's solution to the problem was to take the older nurse off meds and put Joy on them instead.

Mostly though, Karon and Joy, like all the other nurses, dealt with these incidents and then pushed them aside, hoping to forget them. When they were unhappy with their jobs they reminded themselves that everyone is sometimes discontent, that no job is perfect. When they felt mistreated by an administrator or doctor, they blamed the individual, not the system that formed and directed the individual. Karon had wanted to be a nurse since she was a child and had worked as a candy striper as a teenager. Joy, too, had dreamed of a nursing career all her life, had worked as an aide since the age of 15. Everything in their backgrounds had conditioned them for this job. They did not know how to be anything else. They had to make this good, to excel.

So they played by the book, adhered to the rules, followed the idealistic path of the nurse as taught in school. Like good novices in a convent, they accepted the final word from above and always bowed before authority. They lived with the pettiness because they had to. They lived with the little injustices because they believed in the larger good. They swallowed their pride, swallowed their hurt, and told each other stories about the good days, because there were, in truth, many of these. And that's what kept them going. No matter what happened or who said what, in the end, they believed they were performing a necessary, vital service, rather than just shuffling papers in an office somewhere. They valued themselves and hoped, against occasional indications to the contrary, that others also believed in their worth.

That's why the state inspections that year devastated them so much. When they heard from a nurse on another shift how the clerk had been told to update page upon page of hospital procedures by sleight of hand and cunning, cutting off the tops of the pages that held old dates and writing in the new year on the old

46

material, they were angry. Some of the other nurses laughed off the incident. "It's done all the time. People everywhere do this sort of thing." But Joy and Karon didn't laugh. To them this wasn't everywhere, this was here, and it was special. They went home feeling debased, feeling low and dishonest by mere association. They were part of what happened at the hospital. If they had an obligation to keep themselves on the up and up because untoward behavior would reflect poorly on the hospital, then why didn't the hospital have the same obligation to them?

Now they were aware as never before of limits, of tethers tied to their legs and arms and minds. They were aware of a facelessness they'd never experienced before. They had felt important once; now they began to suspect that they really didn't count, not in the eyes of the larger world. "The ever silent nurse," said Karon. "I don't like it." Joy glanced at her friend and said nothing.

chapter three

On Saturday, May 22, 1971, Karon White and Ralph Gibson were married. Their engagement had lasted a year and a half, and finally the wedding that had been postponed since the previous fall—the restaurant Karon wanted for the reception was not available—was to take place No one smiled more than Ralph that day. He was tall, slim, and handsome in his black tux; he had waited a long time for this event and he was happy. Nothing seemed to bother him. No hints of doubt, no questions flashed across his face He looked almost serene. He looked very proud, like a prince who had at last found his princess.

Karon wasn't quite sure how to act. She was happy for Ralph but a little melancholy for her parents. She wanted to be carefree but had had a thousand worries nagging at her the last few weeks. She fussed over the heat that had rolled into the city that dawn She fussed over her hair which a former patient, who was also a beautician, had already fussed over for hours that morning, insisting on coming to the bride's house to do the job so Karon could stay inside in an air-conditioned house. She thought about the food: turkey. Karon had selected that entrée on purpose, wanting something different and therefore memorable. She was terrified that Ralph's ex-wife would show up and had given the best man a detailed description and orders to bar the woman if she tried to crash the party. Karon worried about aunts who liked their martinis a little too much, about the band or the limousine showing up late, about rain falling from a cloudless sky, about the wrong flowers being delivered, about any number of potential disasters.

She needn't have bothered. The wedding was perfect. From

the house to the church to the reception, there were no hitches.

At 4:00 P.M. an Episcopalian minister pronounced Ralph and Karon husband and wife, and opened the door for a new life. Outside the church, Karon's younger brothers passed out rice for the guests to toss and a very pregnant Joy hugged her friend, just as a photographer began engineering the wedding party into his camera lens. Joy had wanted to be one of the five bridesmaids in the high-collared orange dresses, but she had demurred. She was simply too pregnant, she thought, to be in the wedding party. She'd wait with the other guests until the photographer finished, then would drive with Gordon to the reception.

From six until midnight that evening, the 250 wedding guests ate, drank, danced, and toasted some more. They did polkas and cha chas, waltzes and jitterbugs. The men in suits, the women in long dresses or silver pajamas, with earrings dangling and hair billowing. When Ralph and Karon danced, she self-consciously and he like a young Gene Kelly, the guests stepped aside and watched, smiling and talking about how nice the couple looked together. It was a nice wedding.

"Don't forget shoes for the next day," someone had said to Karon before the wedding, but she had forgotten. The following morning, when the Gibsons drove from the local Holiday Inn to Karon's parents' home, the bride was in jeans and peau de soie shoes. No one treated her any differently, and Karon finally began to relax. That afternoon the newlyweds returned to their own apartment, and the next morning, when they flew to Hawaii for a two-week honeymoon, Ralph was still smiling.

＊　　＊　　＊　　＊　　＊

Joy had a miserable summer that year. She'd injured her right leg in a flukey home accident, had had to have surgery, and now was burdened with a heavy plaster cast. She had a newborn infant to care for. Money was tight and Gordon was still drinking. He would come home earlier than usual after work to help put supper on the table but he carried the smell of beer on him and Joy hated him for it.

She'd been ordered to stay off her feet as much as possible and for hours on end, she lay on the couch daydreaming about her life and how it might have been different. Joy saw herself again as the dutiful young daughter of the hard-working, ambitious mother and hard-working, not quite successful, father. As the new kid in the eighth grade at the new school, younger than the rest because she'd been double promoted the year before. Joy saw herself walking into the classroom with her long hair in braids, her skirt full over a starched crinoline, and her white blouse puffy. She remembered how she'd wanted to die when she saw a room full of older boys and of girls in lipstick, straight skirts, and tight sweaters.

What if she hadn't transferred to that school? What if she had gone on later as she'd planned and gotten her bachelor's degree after nurses' training? What if Gordon hadn't been in that car accident on Christmas Eve? They would never have met, he as patient and she as nurse, and he couldn't have persuaded her to accept his proposal and set the date. After nine years of marriage, Joy knew she was losing her husband to alcohol but she didn't know how to win him back. She was trapped, with no way out, so that summer she mourned for herself. Not so much for the years gone by but for the years that were yet to come.

It was such a shame, she thought, such a waste of her life. All she could do, she reasoned, was pour her energies into the rest of her activities and ignore the part of her existence that touched on Gordon. She had been busy before the accident; she would be busier after her recovery. Gazing out the picture window in the living room, Joy vowed never again to waste another minute, never to do anything that was less than constructive. She would do her damndest to make her life as complete as possible and she would accept that and not dream beyond.

When Joy thought of Karon, and she did a lot that summer, she had to shake her head. Here was her friend with the concerned, dutiful husband and yet jealous as could be. To Joy that was ridiculous. So was the free-for-all way Karon spent money. Three hundred dollars for a dress she wore once, then left hanging in the closet. New cars all the time. Expensive vacations. Dinner out every night.

Each of the women disapproved of the way the other was living. "Save your money," Joy told Karon. "Buy a house." Karon didn't want to save money; she didn't want a house. She was motivated by the philosophy that the less you have, the less you can lose in custody court. "Have a baby," Joy suggested. Karon didn't want any children; she'd put in enough time, she figured, babysitting for her younger brothers; she didn't need any more of that kind of responsibility.

In turn, Karon would chide Joy. "You need to get out more" was her favorite and oft-repeated line.

Karon had everything she'd ever dreamed of. She was laughing at her life and afraid of nothing. This was her summer to ride the crest. At home she entertained constantly. At work she envisioned becoming an institution within an institution, of retiring with a gold watch, of being venerated for years of praiseworthy service. Patients seemed to have more respect for her now, as if, married, she was more complete as a person, more acceptable as a woman, more mature as an individual. Now Karon could talk as an authority both to single women and to married women. She had moved up a notch on the developmental ladder society had constructed, and she liked her new perch.

Despite their differences, the two women were developing a strong loyalty to each other. Beneath the differences, they recognized basic similarities, ideas about morality and honor they both shared. That summer, as a result of Joy's accident, a seemingly innocent question came up that would bring them even closer together. For a few weeks Joy required special nursing care at home. Private duty nurses required a minimum of four hours' work; changing Joy's dressings took 20 minutes. Visiting nurses would not provide daily care; Joy's dressing had to be changed every 24 hours. Karon made calls to find a local home care service for her friend but discovered none. Luckily, one of Joy's neighbors was a nurse, and she volunteered to do the job.

But what about people who didn't have such luck? What did

they do? Whom did they turn to in situations like this? Maybe there was a need for a home care nursing service. At least Karon and Joy both agreed it was a good idea and something to think about, before they forgot it and returned to their schedules at General. Joy's leg was healed. She was back in the psych ward again. But the seed for something larger had been planted.

*　*　*　*　*

"No one had time to radio ahead and I didn't know what was coming until the emergency doors flew open and the cart came rolling in. The kid on it was real young and bleeding bad—one of those stupid gang wars. I couldn't believe this was happening in the middle of the afternoon. 'We got another one from the Bucket of Blood on 16th Street,' the cops were yelling. God, everyone was yelling. The intern was yelling to me. I was yelling into the phone, telling surgery to get ready, we were bringing one up."

Karon stopped a minute to light a cigarette. The twenty other women at the table stayed quiet, waiting for the rest of the story. This was an informal gathering, held just weeks after Karon's official five-year nursing school reunion. The first get together had brought back so many memories, Karon decided to organize another smaller party. Not all the women in the small banquet room were her former classmates. Joy was there, for one, and so were two other coworkers from General. But they were all nurses; that was the only qualification for tonight's party. They were nurses talking about their years in nursing. This was not an evening for complaints, but rather one for memorable stories. The episode Karon was relating was from her first experience working in a hospital emergency room as a senior student nurse. "Then the cops brought in another guy, another kid. We almost had a riot in the place. There were so many people mobbing the entrance, the police had to call for reinforcements. They were all really mad, they thought the cops had shot the kids. Turns out, then, that the victims were from rival gangs. I was standing right between them

52

when the one suddenly sits up, looks at the other guy and says, 'That's the one who stabbed me.' And the second one said, 'Yeah, well he's the guy who shot me.'"

"Remember, your first patient who died?" one of the nurses asked, and of course they all did. Karon's had been a stroke victim who seemed well on her way to recovery the morning of the fateful day. "Your mother is much better, you can come see her this afternoon," the young student nurse had told the patient's daughter on the phone. Then Karon had left for fifteen minutes to attend a special clinical conference. When she returned, the woman's daughter was in the hall screaming—she'd just been told her mother was dead. "I was in such shock," Karon told the gathering, "I couldn't even remove the equipment. The medical students did it for me. Then they held the treatment papers for me to sign."

Joy's first death was perhaps the most tragic: an 11-year-old boy who'd been severely burned when a lighted match fell into his boots at a picnic. He never had a chance, as the flames roared up engulfing his body. "Only his face was okay," Joy explained. "It wasn't touched at all." But he couldn't talk, he could just barely open and close his eyes. If the boy survived, doctors said, they'd have to amputate both legs. Within days, however, the young boy died. "His body lay in the room for four hours before anyone could move it," Joy went on. "No one could find his parents; they were divorced and hard to contact." Joy was just a student at the time and had worked closely with the burn victim on the pediatrics ward. She was given the rest of the day off, told to go out and try not to think about it.

There were many dramatic stories told that night, some that hardly seemed believable, but all true. One was about a boy accidentally shot in the face. The bullet had entered the corner of the victim's right eye, traveled through his skull, miraculously missing the brain, and then had lodged just behind the skin at the nape of the neck. From there, it was easily extracted. Another about a six-month-old baby girl who'd been raped and had to have emergency surgery to repair the damage that had been done to

53

her fragile, tiny body. About the gout patient who'd been given a new test medication and whose skin had fallen off. About the man whose penis had been partially bitten off by a neighbor's dog. About the bisexual female psych patient who went out on a pass, had relations with a man, then returned to the ward where she allegedly impregnated her lesbian lover.

Karon talked about a young child whose arm had been so badly mangled in a washing machine his mother refused to have anything to do with him. She let him lie for three years in a hospital, until finally a state agency took over as the boy's guardian and placed the child in a foster home. Then Karon told about the time a baby was stolen from the maternity ward of another hospital; about the strict rule that went into effect at her hospital immediately after the incident, requiring that someone be present in the nursery at all times; and how because of this rule she just happened to be on hand when a baby began to choke and was able to save its life. "Then once by accident, I spilled the Gentian violet I was using on the cord and dyed a baby blue from the waist down just before it was to go home," she said. "Thank God, it wasn't harmful." And everyone laughed.

There were, of course, the famous sponge stories: how three sponges were lost in surgery and everyone feared they had been sewn up inside a patient. (They hadn't been, the staff discovered after x-raying the patient.) How an intern once walked out of the operating room with a sponge clinging to his cuff and the nurses on duty had had to search for an hour before tracing the missing material to the men's washroom. "Remember the time we listened to the World Series in surgery?" one nurse asked. "How about when Dr. Roberts cut the intern's finger by accident, then let the patient lie there while he sewed up the wound," another interjected. "Or the public aid patient with the perforated bladder—no one said anything, even though she had an elevated temperature. They just sent her to county hospital," a third recalled.

On they went. Joy telling about the dying King of the Gypsies and how his 300 followers invaded the hospital corridors and sat in mourning for his passing. Karon relating how frightened she and the other student nurses had been during Martin Luther King's famous march on the city. "We were in the heart of the ghetto and all these people were outside our dorm threatening to toss Molotov cocktails through our windows."

Everyone had a story from the record-breaking blizzard of '67 that dropped 36 inches of snow on Chicago in less than 24 hours, paralyzing the city. Many of the nurses, stranded at home, did first aid on their block and delivered babies down the streets. Karon and her student group had worked extra shifts, doubled up in the nurses' residence to make room for the doctors marooned at the hospital, and had stood with flashlights in a snow-covered park. They had to light the spot where a helicopter would land, bringing in a pregnant woman in labor whom the police would carry on an ironing board to the emergency room entrance.

Lightly, the women moved from one subject to another, one memory to the next. They talked about the patient who thought he was a fire engine, and another, a hydrocephalic, who survived delicate brain bypass surgery, then caught a cold and died from the pneumonia that set in. About patients who smuggled food in before surgery, thinking they were outsmarting the rules and not realizing they were putting themselves in danger of choking in the operating room. They discussed patient abuse of nurses and all nodded as Karon told about the first man she'd ever given a bath to. "I had just finished and was checking his blood pressure when he stuck his hand into my uniform," she said. "I was so startled I didn't know what to do; I just knew I couldn't report this to my supervisor. Then I was assigned to the same man for another week—he'd requested me—and the only way I could cope was to draw an imaginary line around his bed and never step across it, because I didn't want to get within his reach. It ended up, I was standing behind his right shoulder to give him a bath!"

There was a story from psych about a male patient who began sending threatening letters to the nursing staff after his release from the hospital. "Once he got up to seven on the elevator and stood outside staring in the window," said Karon. "I talked to the supervisor but she said not to worry and not to say anything. They took the letters and wouldn't give them back and wouldn't notify the police. They were just afraid the hospital would get bad publicity. It didn't matter about us, right? Who cares if this guy is dangerous or not? Two weeks later he gets arrested right out in front of the hospital. He was trying to screw a telephone pole!"

The nurses compared the teaching hospitals where they'd had their clinical training to the community hospitals most now worked in. The former, they decided, provided better patient care, had more knowledgeable doctors on staff, and should be the hospitals of choice.

Then they moved on to the tales of doctors they'd dated (Joy had had the misfortune of going out with an MD who exposed himself on their first—and last—date), memories of doctors whose work they respected and bedside manner they admired, and stories about doctor/nurse conflicts. "I remember hearing a doctor chewing out this nurse once," Karon said. "He was screaming at her, threatening to report her. 'What is your name?' he kept saying. 'Tell me your name.' She just glared at him and yelled back, 'You can call me Nurse!' Then she turned her back and walked away."

Another time, when a fly was buzzing about in the operating room, the surgeon became furious at the scrub nurse. He blamed her for the problem and literally threw her out of the room. "We had an older MD who used to harass the student nurses and even some of the nurses in the hospital. He was always playing grab-ass and looking for the sexual favors, and if the nurses complained he'd have them fired." Karon went on. "Finally the other doctors got mad because all their best nurses were being dumped because of this guy. One day they hired a prostitute for him and rented a room downtown and told him to go get his fill. He never showed, and after that the message to him from the other doctors was either to put up or shut up. And he shut up."

There were memories too of doctors noted for their callous

treatment of patients, like the story about the one who was angry because a woman refused to breastfeed her baby. "Well, I'll schedule surgery and we'll cut them off then if you're not going to use them for what they were meant," he'd said, sending the woman into hysterics. Or the intern who came into a young girl's room and asked point blank whether she wanted to be a man or a woman, because she "had both inside her." Occasionally, a story of neglect rose to the surface. "We had a woman who'd just delivered," one nurse said. "And she started to develop this huge hematoma. We called the OB man several times but he said we shouldn't worry. A few hours later the patient died." Then another nurse took the floor. "Well, what about these anesthesiologists who set up six patients at once, then leave residents to take care of them after they're under. We had a guy like that once; he'd bill all the patients for his full services, even though he didn't do the work."

The nurses talked about patients who gave their children bizarre names (one christened her twins Syphilis and Gonorrhea after she overheard two nurses use the terms; another dubbed her child Fa-male-é, for female). They talked about people's misconceptions of medicine (one patient scheduled for a hysterectomy was found in bed with her husband the night before surgery—the couple thought they wouldn't be able to have sex after the woman's operation. Another came in saying she had fireballs in her uterus—they were really fibroid tumors).

And they talked about Richard Speck, the man convicted of murdering eight Chicago student nurses during the time most of them were students. Some of the women present that evening had shared their psychiatric training with one or two of the victims; nurses from Karon's class had been pallbearers at three of the funerals; and Ralph, Karon's husband, had been one of the policemen assigned to guard Speck after his capture.

For their own sanity, the women could not dwell for long on the morbid. Karon quickly jumped to another memory, the time she scrubbed with a doctor about to perform trigeminal nerve surgery. "He said he'd never done it before and had only one hour to read up on the procedure. 'Hope I don't paralyze this man's face,' he said as he went in."

And she told about the time an orderly and a LPN named Edie gave a patient an enema. "The nurse kept calling the orderly 'honey' while this man pleaded, 'No more, no more.' No way, says Edie. She's gonna show him who's boss. 'Honey, we have to shove it in until it comes out his ears,' she kept saying. 'It's a "three H" enema. Make it high, hot, and a helluva lot.' The orderly was standing there holding the bag when suddenly Edie gives it a whack to force the rest of the soapy water out and bang! It all backfires and the nurse and the orderly are both splattered with the stuff. 'Oh shit, honey,' she said."

Then Joy related the incredible tale of the fecal sample sent by mistake to a physician's home rather than to his office. "It was just before Christmas and when this box arrives 'Do Not Open' they all thought it was a Christmas present from a patient. So they put it under the tree and it sat there for a week, smelling up the house, until on Christmas Day the doctor opened it."

And the two friends told the other nurses how Joy had been a student nurse in Obstetrics at Memorial Hospital when Karon's middle brother, John Hill, a foster child taken in by her family as an infant, had been born there. "That means I was 13 when our paths first crossed," said Karon. "And now look, we're working together."

By the end of the evening, as these gatherings go, the nurses were in a sentimental mood. They had just spent hours talking and laughing about their lives, reaffirming their roles, putting a little starch back into collars inevitably wilted by the sweat of hard work. When Karon stood and said the last few words, there was hardly a dry eye in the room. What she was going to read them, she said, was an anonymous poem written during wartime. She'd first heard it at the black banding ritual that had marked the end of her formal clinical training. The doctor who chaired the ceremony had recited it as a tribute to the graduating nurses.

Ever since it had been one of Karon's favorites. It went like this:

> There's a rose that grows in no man's
> land
> And she's beautiful to see.
> She's the one red rose
> A sick man knows,
> She's the work of the master's hand.
> Through my life's great curse
> Stood a smiling nurse—
> She's the rose of no man's land.

chapter four

*F*or a long time it was difficult for Karon to understand Joy's shyness around men. Karon was the kind of woman who'd always liked men, felt comfortable with them, and enjoyed sharing their company. She had been her father's darling and mentor to her three younger brothers. She was accustomed to men, enjoyed their attention, especially liked talking to them.

Not so with Joy who avoided contact as much as possible. If the two nurses were at the station together and a doctor came by, Karon would strike up a conversation while Joy would turn away, as if afraid to have any dealings with the man. In fact, fear did play a part in her behavior; it was fear of Gordon, whose jealousy was maddening. One time after they were first married Gordon had called Joy at the hospital where she was working and had had to wait because she was on another line with a patient's doctor. He'd been furious, incredulous that his wife was talking to a man. "What do you think I do?" she'd exploded at him. "It's part of my job." He'd only sneered his derision at her.

Later, if she was ten minutes late returning from the store, Gordon always knew why, and the reason always involved a man. Joy remembered the day her husband had come in the front door and announced that he'd been watching the house and had seen the men walking in. Another time, after a winter snowstorm, Joy had given a young orderly a ride to a nearby train station. He had taken his tie off when they left the hospital and Joy didn't realize until she had gotten home that he'd dropped it on the car floor. She was petrified. Gordon must not find that tie in her car, so Joy threw it in the garbage. The next day the orderly asked if she'd found it and she lied to him, said she'd never seen it. Because her truths were lies to Gordon, Joy had no defense against his accusations. She could only try to protect herself, and the only way she knew was to avoid as much as possible all contact with men. There would be one exception: John Castro, MD.

Karon had first seen Dr. Castro in a hospital elevator. Then one day she was standing by the nurses' station when he walked past. Karon had heard a lot about Dr. Castro and was inclined to believe every word. "His name is John. They call him Don John, and you can't work here for long without finding out why."

John Castro was a handsome man; he said hello with his eyes, smiled with his face, and had a way of seeming to edge closer without actually moving at all. Karon watched him, fascinated. He looked like he'd just stepped out of a finishing school where male models are trained to act like doctors. The white coat hung just right, playing up the tan and the dark eyes. The steps were properly hurried, the brow furrowed into a nice combination of concern and authority. Only he knew the jargon too. Doctor's words poured from his mouth in precise school-taught English and when he listened, it was the way a doctor did, an intent gaze moving from the speaker's face to the floor while the head nodded absently.

"Not bad," one of the new, temporary nurses said as Dr. Castro stepped off down the hall to his consultation.

"Certainly very interesting," Karon replied.

Up and down the corridor female patients tittered, but the doctor didn't notice, or at least he seemed not to. He was all business, a busy internist here to see a patient with symptoms of a gallbladder attack. To Dr. Castro, time was everything and he didn't believe in wasting any. He couldn't afford to, Joy and Karon later learned, because of the needy patients he'd sometimes treat without charge.

Ten minutes later John Castro was back. He walked directly up to the station where Karon, alone, pecked at a typewriter.

"False alarm, but better to be sure."

61

She nodded and looked back to her work, aware of the absence of the sound of footsteps moving away toward the door

"I think you should have dinner with me sometime," Dr. Castro said.

"I don't think so. I'm married." Karon was cool, practiced, and taking no chances.

"Is that important?"

"It is to me."

She gave him one of her aloof, detached looks. He watched her intently, smiled, then gave a brief formal nod.

"Very well, just trying to be friendly." And he was gone, vanished beyond the gray metal door, off to a floor full of questioning patients, to a luxurious home and his own seven children, to a private office filled with more patients, to a beautiful wife, to a girlfriend perhaps, or maybe just to a small room with a single bed where he might lie down a minute. Karon didn't know which, but she knew any one of them could have been accurate.

She hadn't taken the proposition, if it could be called that, seriously. In fact, she told Ralph about it the next day, laughing and pleased. Men who asked her out were not threats; they were simply vehicles by which she reaffirmed her own attractiveness. To her, this was a game, a ritual of life, and if princes or kings paid her the attention, so much the better. They'd get nothing out of it, and she'd have the pleasure of knowing she'd turned a royal head. Since there were no kings around, doctors would have to do, and handsome doctors would do better than plain ones. Dr. Castro was a new face on the block, a new challenge. He might want to be an admirer, but she would turn him into a friend. For her, that was important, to be his equal in that one sense if in no other way.

One of the gauges by which Karon measured people was how true they were to themselves. Dr. Castro hit the mark perfectly.

"He knows what he's got and he flaunts it," she explained to Joy later over cold hamburgers.

"He's an arrogant bastard," the other nurse responded. "I was

62

on duty at St. Vincent's when he came in once. He acted like he owned the world."

They had their first argument that night over Dr. Castro. Karon agreed the man was arrogant, but defended what she saw as his right to be so. "He's good at what he does and a lot of people aren't. He works hard. He can't help it if he's good-looking. And besides he had to swim all the way from Cuba and anyone who can do that deserves to be arrogant."

But Joy wasn't in a generous mood. For once in her life she was beginning to suspect that hard work wasn't its own reward. She was tired of feeling left behind, tired of people who looked important because they were standing on other people's shoulders. She didn't believe Karon about Dr. Castro's hard work and thought of him only as a privileged playboy who got where he was by luck.

"He fell asleep one time leaning against a wall talking to someone on the phone, he was so overworked." Karon tried to bolster the doctor's image by repeating a story she'd heard.

"Was he fired? Did anyone throw him out of the hospital—no. That's what they would have done to us," Joy replied. Then as an afterthought. "For $100,000 a year, I'd fall asleep against walls exhausted too."

Eventually, however, Joy came around and began to like the man. She'd been put off by Dr. Castro's slick veneer, but now saw that there was more substance behind it than she'd thought. She heard him ask Karon for recommendations on which psychiatrists were the most reliable; she began to overhear positive comments about his patient care. When she saw he had a sense of humor, he appeared much more human to her.

One day Dr. Castro came up to the psych ward with another man, whom he introduced as his brother, a cardiologist. "I told him what an impressive arrangement you have here, that he should tour the facility, with your permission, of course."

Half an hour later when the two left, after much talking from Dr. Castro and much head nodding from his brother, the internist stopped in the doorway, flashed a big grin, and saluted.

"He is my brother, yes. But I'll bet this is the first time you ladies have met someone who drives tomato trucks in Florida. Buenos dias."

Shortly afterward, Karon asked the doctor to help her arrange a blind date for a friend, another nurse.

"She was supposed to get married right after Ralph and I did, but it was called off, very suddenly," Karon explained. "You must know someone, a nice handsome doctor."

Dr. Castro promised a good-looking surgeon. He delivered a hobbling, bent, middle-aged doctor who was recovering from a recent hernia operation. Karon and Joy watched horrified from the hospital lobby as their friend helped her doctor-date into his car. They'd made contingency plans, of course, to have her paged at the restaurant because of an "emergency," but Dr. Castro had his own bag of tricks. He'd convinced the other doctor to make reservations at an unknown spot. All evening the nurse and the doctor sat together. He had a fetish about germs and constantly excused himself to go to the bathroom and wash his hands. The nurse was furious and the next day told Karon and Joy about her awful date.

The two cornered Dr. Castro, going at him until he finally apologized. Karon didn't think twice about chewing out the doctor over his dirty trick. But for Joy it was a new experience. She didn't know she had it in her. After that incident, it became much easier, more natural, for Joy to joke and talk with Dr. Castro, rather than turn to a file or a book whenever he appeared on the floor. But she still felt uncomfortable making her way into conversations with other men, and usually left that to Karon.

*   *   *   *   *

Neither Joy nor Karon could pinpoint when the restlessness had begun. They had become aware of it slowly, over an extended period of time. Initially, it was the minor aggravations that had gotten to them—lying to get a food tray for a late admit, arguing over the sour soup the patients refused to eat and the kitchen refused to replace. One day they stopped laughing when patients asked, "Are you the maid?" and visitors blandly inquired if they had to have graduated from high school to be nurses. They began to get angry when they overheard coworkers identify themselves by saying, "Oh, we're just nurses." The qualification, the thoughtless putdown hurt.

Clear and painful memories began to haunt them. Their late-night talk sessions became more serious now as they indulged in bitter recollections. Joy told Karon about the Christmas her nursing class was ordered downtown to sing carols for sailors at a USO. "What the hell were we doing entertaining the Navy?" she demanded, as much of herself as of her friend. "Do you know not one of us even questioned it? We just went. Stood there like a bunch of fools and sang our hearts out. Everyone thought it was cute; so did we."

Karon told Joy about how her class had to leave the doors to their rooms open two inches every evening during study hours. "There were mirrors bolted to the walls across from the desks," she explained. "When the monitors came around they could just peek in and see our reflections in the mirrors. They probably don't even do that in convents."

Together they remembered the nursing school rules, instituted not for rational reasons, but simply to instill in them a sense of obedience and a feeling of humility. They had both been taught, for example, never to address a physician directly, but to speak only when spoken to. They had learned early in their training to walk down the sides of halls, never in the center. They had been required to wear shoes with a specified number of holes for the laces and to make sure that the hems of their skirts were a certain number of inches from the floor. They had been told they could not socialize with medical students, and, if they wished to marry, they could do so only during the last six months of training. They had not been allowed to wear their uniforms outside the hospital setting, and they had been told repeatedly that the term *nurse* originally had meant servant.

Each time the two women ate together, drove together, went shopping together, they talked. The more they talked, the more they began to understand their situation, although sex as an issue hadn't entered into the picture yet. Karon and Joy sincerely believed that being women had nothing to do with their plight. They were convinced the problem stemmed from some undetermined flaw in the nursing profession, some intrinsic weakness that needed to be rooted out and corrected. So they worked even harder on the job, signed up for the educational courses the hospital offered, and tried to be even better nurses.

The more they tried, the more disturbed they were by the insensitivity and sometimes incompetence they witnessed around them. Suddenly, they had no patience for the intern who refused to run an EKG on a patient with severe chest pain and who, once he capitulated, admitted he couldn't read the tape anyway. None either for the psychiatrist who turned a quiet, peaceful man into a monster by telling him to "act out his anger" however he wanted to.

When a fish tank appeared on the psych floor, they were incredulous. "No combs, no nothing, but they put a glass fish tank out in the middle of the floor! What do they think this is, nursery school?" Karon complained. Two hours later, they rushed a patient to the emergency room with blood spurting from his temples. The man had run head on into the tank, smashing it into a dozen pieces and leaving dead fish, water, gravel, and seaweed for the staff to clean up.

Karon and Joy realized the heavy responsibility that they as nurses had over the well-being of the patients, and the almost zero input they had into decision-making that bore directly on patient care.

"It's ludicrous," they told Ralph one evening over diet drinks. "We see what's going on. We report to the doctor. He almost always says, 'Well, what do you think?' So we refer to lab reports or to what happened the day before yesterday with the same patient, and we make a suggestion. Then he turns our answer into his order and we have to go back and do exactly what we wanted to do in the first place. If things go well, he gets the credit. If things go wrong, he can always say the nurse gave him incorrect information. We're there to take blame, but we never get any credit. When's the last time you heard someone say, 'Who was your nurse?' They always ask, 'Who was your doctor?' We *are* a bunch of servants."

Then they went back to work, because they had no choice, even as the stories piled up. More incidents from the past popped into their minds. Like the time years before when Karon and another student nurse sat for hours in a hot, sweaty room tending a five-year-old victim of meningitis. They talked to her, bathed her with alcohol solutions, and checked the IVs and the respirator, monitoring her condition and praying until, nearly six hours later, her vital signs became stable. The crisis had passed. The child, a tiny black girl, was resting comfortably when a medical student came in to relieve them. Exhausted and soaked, with their hair clinging to their necks, their uniforms dirty and sticking to their backs, they went down to the cafeteria to rest. Only minutes passed before word reached them that the girl had just died. The respirator had malfunctioned and the medical student, considered superior to them in every way, hadn't known how to reset it.

"You know, we couldn't say or do a thing about it." Joy knew. She'd walked the same narrow line. She could remember when nurses weren't allowed to tell patients that a tablet was an aspirin. "They'd ask, 'What is that?' and we were supposed to say we didn't know, or suggest they ask their doctor. Some stupid nurse, huh, giving out medicine she couldn't identify!"

Joy vividly recalled one patient, an older woman, emaciated, worn down with cancer, in almost constant pain. "My God, she wanted to talk, but I couldn't talk to her because her doctor hadn't ordered 'counseling.' She'd ask me, 'Am I dying?' and I'd have to say, 'Oh, don't be silly, I'll give you this shot and you'll feel better.' An hour and a half later and she was in pain again. She knew she was dying. Her family knew, and so did I. I felt like such a hypocrite. You know, you can only say you don't know so many

67

times before you have to choke the words out of your mouth." Joy poured another teaspoonful of sugar into her half-empty, half-cold cup of coffee and stirred it aimlessly. After a moment she looked at Karon. Karon dragged on a cigarette and looked away.

"You should quit smoking. It's no good for you."

"I know. I know, believe me I know. But it's my only vice."

It was after midnight when they each got home and fell into bed for an uneasy sleep. Joy had been through periods in her life of dreading her tomorrows, but for Karon this was a new experience. She didn't like it.

Not long afterward, a fire broke out on 7E during the second shift. Joy had seven patients out on pass; they were swimming in the clear chlorinated water of the YMCA pool when the dark billows of smoke began seeping from a patient's room (he'd set the drapes on fire with a book of contraband matches—this, after tossing his roommate s money and shaver in the toilet). With only one orderly to help, Karon rounded up her 23 charges and in minutes had them safely outside the locked door, standing excitedly to one side as the firemen rushed past. Damage was confined to the one room, but the scent of smoke hung heavy in the air, making the unit uninhabitable for a few hours.

"Everyone is behaving so nicely, let's reward them with dinner in the lobby," one of the administrators suggested.

Karon wouldn't hear of it. She knew the patients were under control only because of their initial fear and her strict discipline. A party atmosphere in a free, open area could be disastrous. She won, and dinner was served in a small lounge instead.

The next morning the Director of Nurses sent for Karon. "You did a fine job yesterday. You are to be commended for it. I just want you to know we appreciate your service."

All her life Karon had sought and thrived on such praise. From her family, her teachers, her bosses. To her, it was more important that people respect her than like her. She knew this and realized she should have been thrilled with the director's compliment. Instead, she was depressed, because rather than comfort,

68

the words had disturbed, had pointed up another limitation.

"There's nowhere to go, not really," she told Joy. "I could have saved the whole place from certain death and they'd have given me a pat on the back and that's all. Oh, if I'm good and hang around forever, I might get to be a supervisor. Maybe. But chances are, ten years from today I'll be doing exactly what I'm doing now." It's funny, she thought to herself, that's just what I always wanted. Now it doesn't sound so good.

Ten years from then Joy would be 42 years old. Her oldest daughter would be in college, her youngest son would be entering junior high school. Life would go on and she would still be a nurse, just a nurse. The thought haunted Joy on the drive home, as she tooled her brown station wagon through the streets; it followed her through the dimly lit rooms of her house all the way into the bedroom; it played games with her dreams. The next morning, even before she opened her eyes, it was banging at the door to her mind.

Joy had always thought that being a nurse was enough, was something to be truly proud of. Now she realized that her initial concept of nurse had been different from the reality as she'd lived it. In the concept, there were always more plateaus, new horizons, ways to grow. Ten years from now she would be a nurse emptying bedpans, fluffing pillows, and taking orders. She'd be an older nurse, a more experienced nurse, but still just a nurse.

Now incidents and comments that had once amused Joy began to anger her. She recalled all the times she'd heard people talk about how "fast" nurses were. She remembered the patient who'd stuck his hand right into the top of a nurse's uniform and how the residents and doctors had laughed. She saw again the young nurse being reprimanded because a patient had pulled her into his bed. The more Joy thought about the situation, the more clear the picture. The joke was always on the nurse, who was almost always the woman. For years nursing had been Joy's escape from marriage. But her position as a woman, she realized, was no better at the hospital than it was at home.

Through the fall of 1972, Joy and Karon grappled with their problems. They talked in circles, in loud angry voices, in quiet desperate tones. They talked about what they knew until they were sick of it; then they talked about what they didn't know and got lost and had to retreat to familiar ground. They were two women in need of a new dream and they couldn't find one. There were plenty of outrageous fantasies, but Joy and Karon were too practical for these. They needed something they could prod and poke at, something at least slightly plausible. Time and again, they got discouraged and rushed back to the security of what they were and what they had. But even fate seemed against them, because inevitably something would happen to jolt them out of their assumed complacency.

One day Karon came in with a clipping from a newspaper. The item, only a paragraph long, told about a nurse in California who was taking blood pressures at a shopping center. She'd set up a card table and chairs in a corner of the parking lot, worked strictly on her own, and made $20,000 in one year.

"So? What's that supposed to mean?" Joy had just finished reading the story. They were sitting at the station, checking assignments for the day.

"Nothing, except that some nurse is using her noodle to get ahead and we're sitting here and doing nothing."

Joy swirled her chair, turning her back on her friend. She shrugged her shoulders and reached toward a pile of folders that needed to be updated.

"Think about it," Karon said.

"About what?"

"Something. Anything. Don't ask me. Just think about it. What we might be able to do."

"Karon, I've never done anything else. Give me a break." As she spoke, Joy turned around again. Her face set and exasperated, but with something in her eyes that said she'd heard and understood every word of the conversation.

"You never had a baby either, not until you had your first one. Now look at you."

70

"Sure, old baby machine, that's what everyone's going to start calling me." But Joy laughed as she spoke and with a grudging nod agreed that yes, she would think about it.

Of course, neither of them did. They didn't have time. Nor did they take the time. Not until other events piled in on them. The first was Joy's encounter with a neighbor, an innocent chat over the backyard fence about what was new and who was doing what. The neighbor's daughter, a high school junior, had just gotten a part-time job as a cashier at a local supermarket, part of a large Midwestern chain.

"Oh, she's just delighted. She feels so responsible and Bill and I both think this will be real good for her," the neighbor chirped. "She's such a good girl and we're so proud. You know how some kids are today." Her eyebrows shot up and her face took on that set-in-cement look of disapproval parents learn to master early in their careers. "It's just wonderful. And the pay! Let me tell you, they didn't pay us like this." Now the neighbor leaned over pretending an aura of confidence but really wishing a crowd could hear her news. "$5.50 an hour." Joy almost dropped her garbage. "Next year, it'll be $6.50. Isn't that just marvelous?"

Joy was furious, but managed to smile in her neighbor's direction before mumbling something about getting her daugher to dancing class and her dog to the vet. During the short trip to the alley and back again to the house, Joy was so angry she could barely think. Figures, large neon-lit figures, pressed at her: $5.50, $6.50, flashing and taunting her. No, no, she argued to herself, throwing a frying pan into the sink. That can't be right. That can't possibly be right. It's not fair! God, how it's not fair. These kids are getting $5.50 an hour for a job a moron could do!

When Joy's anger finally passed, the despair rolled in. Slowly, she walked through her house, looking at the old furniture, the pictures, the things one uses and seeks for comfort. They weren't bad, but they weren't all that great, either. To get this far, though, had taken the best effort she and Gordon had. She thought of her children and their future, the money that would be needed; she heard herself saying no to them, no for music lessons and no for

71

new bikes and no for a new coat, things she hadn't had to deny yet and didn't ever want to. In her room Joy stood in front of the open closet and stared languidly at her uniforms. She hated them, wanted to tear them up, use them for floor rags, fly one over the house as a flag so the world would know a fool lived there.

When she dressed for work that day, Joy did so with her eyes closed. She brushed her long hair without looking in the large mirror over the dresser. In the bathroom, she smeared on eye shadow and foundation in hurried, nasty jabs, keeping her eyes turned up toward the ceiling. She didn't want to see herself, didn't want to look at herself as a nurse.

At the hospital, she was cool and distant, polite to patients but without her usual warmth and openness. Karon assumed she and Gordon had had a fight and let her be. She wasn't surprised when, around 10:30, Joy asked her to go out for a snack later but she was surprised by the conversation.

"How much do you make?" There was an edge to Joy's voice, a hard edge rarely heard.

Karon hesitated. There were things you didn't talk about. Your husband's love-making was one. Money was another.

"Karon, I asked you a question. How much?"

"Five-ninety-two." Joy was her friend. They worked together. Why shouldn't she know?

"I make five-fifty. Karon, I've been a nurse for more than ten years. I went to school for this. I paid to learn this business. I have to deal with a lot of nasty stuff at work. Sometimes, I even save lives. There are actually people who need me. And I earn the same as some 16-year-old kid who works the cash register at National Star. I don't understand it. I honestly don't understand what's going on, I . . ." And her voice trailed off. She sat for a moment with her head down and her hands clenched, then she looked up.

"Can you figure this out? Do you know what's wrong?"

Karon shook her head. "We're getting screwed, that's all I can tell you. We are getting screwed."

Silence again.

72

"Is that really true? Are you sure?"

"Yes, yes, I'm sure. Something to do with the union. We, of course, have no union. Sometimes I wonder if we have any sense."

The talk that evening came in spurts, then gave way to angry looks and nervous gestures, with Karon either smoking or drumming her fingers and Joy playing with the sugar packets on the table. She'd remove them one by one from the round white bowl in front of her, inspect both sides, then carefully slide them back into place. Perhaps if they'd known that other women in other cities all over the country were having similar conversations, they would have felt less at sea. But they didn't know. They felt alone in their anger, in their feeling of being used and abused. They could turn only to each other for comfort. Even then, they realized neither could really help the other since each was in exactly the same situation.

The money problem was not a simple one. Karon and Joy knew that nursing was no avenue to great wealth, but they always thought they would be paid what they were worth and that, beyond money, other compensations, such as the sense of being needed and admired, would be theirs. "We aren't being paid what we're worth," said Joy. "We're being paid what they can get away with paying us. A few pennies and lots of nice-sounding words that no one even believes anymore, except us. We think we're so high and mighty because we're nurses. You know what we are? The fall guys in a big con job. As if to pay us more would be to insult our profession! What a joke. What a big, stupid joke. You can't even say the words *nurse* and *money* in the same sentence. That means you're greedy or you don't care." Sitting there in a quiet, almost deserted restaurant, huddled over a formica-top table, the women felt they had been had.

Over the next couple of months Joy and Karon did some hard thinking, talking, and analyzing. They came up with two major weaknesses in their profession. One was that a great number of nurses worked only part-time and seemed to consider nursing a job, not a career. Most nurses didn't want to rock the boat; their husbands urged them not to make waves, not take a chance on getting fired. Stuck in this spot, nurses tended to talk about problems, never to act on them, the second major shortcoming.

"Do you have any idea the number of times we've sat around and bitched? All of us. At General, at Northeast, at every hospital I've ever worked at," Joy said one evening soon after. "When I think back on it, I can't come up with one instance of a nurse fighting back. Not ever. That's really pathetic. What a bunch of chumps we are."

And on it went. Around them at work other nurses continued in the old vein, and while Karon and Joy did so ostensibly, too, they also did more. The hospital was still vital to them, still the focus of their activities, but now they looked at it through more critical eyes and interpreted events through a broader focus. Together, they came to the same conclusion: at some point they would have to move on. To what, or where, or how, they did not know. They were terrified by the prospect of regrets, the kind they heard from so many people who look back and say "What if?" And they were angry enough over the stifling rules and regulations they encountered to keep looking for the chance they needed to be something a little more than what they were. Joy was ready for something new entirely; Karon simply wanted to expand her scope. But both wanted some indefinable something.

Although they didn't realize it at the time, one of the final straws that would force them into action was provided by a friendly old drunk. He'd been on a three-week binge and was brought to the ER by the police paddy wagon. His clothes were damp and mildewy, stinking of sweat and vomit; his body was in even worse condition, covered with large draining wounds and the accumulated filth of skid row. Rather than treat him downstairs, the ER sent him up to 7E for observation and DT treatment.

Without a doctor's orders, the nurses could do nothing for the man. They could not give him a bath. They could not take a

74

culture of his wounds—a simple procedure of swabbing the fluid, putting a sample of it in a tube, and sending it to the lab. They could not even order a general diet or give the man an aspirin for his headache, even though he claimed always to take them on his own.

Karon wanted permission to start working with the patient; more than that she wanted the resident to check him out. The only way she could get the doctor up to see the man was to bug him. So she made eight separate calls, each time seeking an okay for a different procedure. The tactic worked, and the doctor finally came to the psych ward. Karon had used the rules to achieve her goal, but later when she thought about it, the entire incident played back like a bad dream.

"We're always forced to go through all that with a patient, calling to get permission for everything," she complained to Joy. "It's like we don't have any brains. I feel like a television screen or a camera passing on images. I remember one time I had to watch all night while a patient had those typical reactions to Thorazine. His neck just kept getting stiffer and his eyes drooped more and more, all night. He kept saying, 'Nurse, please, help me. This is driving me crazy.' I had the Artane to reverse the reaction right there—God, I've given it dozens of times—but I couldn't reach his doctor. He had gone somewhere. I don't know where. And I had to just do nothing. I am really getting tired of that, and I'm scared too, about what it's going to do to me. You know, when I first started I didn't worry about stuff like this. I saw the older nurses, like nuns, all meek and practically bowing and scraping, and I thought, boy, that will never be me. But it happens. It's happened a little to you. I don't think that's good. I don't think it's good at all."

They were drinking diet colas again, two familiar faces in a familiar spot. The waitress knew them by name, as did the cook and the owner. Whenever the two of them came in, there was the usual spate of teasing and chatter. How's this, how's that? A few comments on the weather, sometimes on the news. These were people who lived ordinary lives doing routine work. They liked and understood each other and listened sympathetically to each other's gripes, and in their little nighttime enclave had created a small world of their own.

Joy and Karon were plotting for a bigger world, but nothing specific yet. There was talk, sure, but who didn't talk? The cook of opening his own place, the owner of retiring to a Greek island and his own health spa, the waitress of becoming a singer and stand-up comic, and Joy and Karon of doing something different. Sure, sure, everyone nodded. Sounds great, don't it? Yeah, well, good luck, we'll send roses. That kind of stuff. Then they'd turn around and stick their dreams in their hearts and their hands back in the soapy dishwater. The danger was that some day they'd stop dreaming entirely. Then the means to an end became the goal, and lives that had been moved along by some inner sparkle began to stand still and to pale.

"I wonder how many of us will make it," Joy said absently looking at the waitress, the cook, and the restaurant owner, but seeing a wave of people fanning over her life. Her mother had made it, going on at age 50 to become an LPN and fulfill a life's wish. Her father had not. So many of her friends had seemingly given up, so many of the old patients and their relatives, well, she had no way of knowing. She thought of her children and their dreams, because they each had them. She didn't know—who could?—what prompted a mind to think a certain way or to have certain yearnings.

There were times when Joy wasn't even sure if dreams were a blessing or a curse. Times when she hated her own stirrings and despaired the anxiety and worry this ambition brought on. She knew, however, there was no turning back. She and this crazy lady friend of hers were going off somewhere on a great hunt, for a different future. Maybe they wouldn't have to go very far, just a few steps up or sideways. How horrible if they went too far and never could make it back, because after all, their lives weren't so very bad as they were. They were okay, pretty decent lives, really. A lot of people would be happy settling for what they had. But—and here was the bitch of it all—they themselves couldn't any longer. They had been both blessed and cursed, she decided; they had to go on, somewhere.

"I wonder if we'll make it," she said again.

chapter five

In the eight months from February to September, 1973, Joy Catterson and Karon Gibson entered on a course of action that eventually altered completely their status as nurses and touched upon almost every aspect of their lives. Each woman was motivated by a different set of circumstances, but that didn't matter. They joined in a common effort to attain their individual goals. Until, in the long run, what they created became an end in itself, overshadowing all other considerations.

Karon had been fidgety for months. Once summer was over and the apartment complex swimming pool closed for the season, she had little to do between ten o'clock when she woke and 2:30 when she went to work. She couldn't shop every day; she had only one favorite soap opera, and keeping the apartment took only minutes. There were fewer parties now as the friends she and Ralph socialized with began having babies and devoting their energy to their families. Karon had time on her hands and needed a way to fill it.

Joy had a jealous, alcoholic husband in her life and was searching for a way to get out from under his thumb. She thought if she could make more money she'd have more control over her existence. If she could get out of debt and then earn enough on her own to make the house payments, take care of the food bills, and pay for the kids' clothes and schooling, she might be able to pressure Gordon into shaping up—or she might even be able to walk out on him.

Both Joy and Karon were restless. They were looking for something more in their lives. They felt they had chosen their fates and could not alter the essentials, could not become movie stars or millionaires or jet off to London on business. They were nurses. A strange mixture, disillusioned by the medical limbo they were stuck in, nowhere to move or progress. Hurt and confused by a salary structure that demeaned them, yet buoyed by the idea that a nurse in California could take a blood pressure manometer, set up a stand in a parking lot, and have people pay her. My God, they thought, if she can do it, why can't we?

It all seemed so simple and yet so frightening. They knew nothing about the mechanics of setting up a business; they had no training or experience in bookkeeping or billing; they had no connections, no advisers, no models. They didn't understand taxes or insurance or bulk ordering. They weren't even sure what they wanted to do—or if legally they could do anything at all.

Karon began trying to find out. At home every morning, she sat down at the brown dining room table, opened a new orange spiral tablet, and started making phone calls. Each day she'd call a different list of people, and each afternoon she'd tell Joy what she had learned. The Illinois Nurses Association, the Illinois State Medical Society, the American Medical Association, and HEW all said no problem, independent nursing was new and largely untried, but could be done. You'll have to incorporate, Karon was told. You'll need a good lawyer. Who's good? she'd ask. No one knew and Karon would begin her telephone calls again, her notebook turning into a network of names and numbers. She was terrified of failing and swore her friend to secrecy. "We'll look like fools if we brag about starting our own practice and then can't do it. We don't say a word until everything is set. I don't want anyone to say we're just blowing a lot of smoke over this."

By the end of February, Karon and Joy had two basic facts to go on. An independent nursing practice was perfectly legal and was within their abilities to establish. They'd have to have $1,000 to get started. Once the money was deposited in a business account, the incorporation was virtually guaranteed and they could start practicing the profession of nursing on their own.

The women kicked around the idea for two months. They whispered about it whenever they were alone together; they talked privately during lunch hours when the patients were busy with friends and relatives. They'd stop for a sandwich after work and again the main topic of conversation was "the business." At home, finally, one would call the other with another worry or question and they'd feed each other's ego and calm each other's fears until 1:00 or 2:00 A.M.

Neither of them was concerned about time conflicts arising between their jobs at General and their own practice. They were permanently scheduled for the afternoon shift and knew their commitment to the hospital fell between set hours: 2:30 P.M. to 11 P.M. for Karon, 3:00 P.M. to 11 P.M. for Joy. The day shift had enough staff either on full- or part-time to cover itself in an emergency; if a substitution was ever needed on days, neither of them would be called to fill in. All those hours in the mornings and early afternoons were theirs, to say nothing of their days off. We could do it, they reasoned, by each working 20 to 25 hours a week in the practice. We'd set certain office hours, maybe three days a week, when people could call for an appointment or come in and be sure of our being in. If we had to, we could schedule patients for the other two days of the week or for one of our free days.

Naively, they planned to do primarily blood pressure measurements, because it seemed the simplest option. If necessary they'd draw blood for premarital exams. The memory of Joy's accident and her difficulty in securing at-home nursing care kept coming back to them, but that was a much more complicated area to think about. They weren't ready for that yet; they didn't want to jump in too far over their heads, if they decided to jump in at all.

The nurses had no idea how the hospital would react to the idea of two of its employees in part-time, independent practice. Joy thought what they did on their free time was no one's business but their own. Karon was sure the hospital wouldn't like it and was worried that General might have some say about the matter. She knew that her partner fantasized of a time when the business

80

would be so successful she could quit the hospital and devote all her energy to the practice. Karon, who had the more prestigious job at General, didn't want to do that. She always thought of the practice—at least for her—as strictly part-time, and so painstakingly kept the two interests separate. She and Joy talked about their situation at work but they made no phone calls and wrote no letters pertaining to the practice when they were in psych. They told none of the other nurses or staff about their idea. They didn't want to share it and didn't want to be accused later of instigating any kind of discord. The safest path for them was a strictly conservative one.

It will be fun to be on our own, they insisted one day. It's impossible, they said the next. It's going to be terrific. It's going to be horrid. Everyone will come to us because we'll be cheaper than doctors. No one will come because they won't trust nurses working on their own. Finally, they decided not to talk about it for a while. Too much uncertainty. Then Joy might start again: "Do you think we should wear uniforms?" or Karon: "I wonder how we'll pay the rent" and off they'd go again.

Both had told their husbands about their idea and had gotten their approval. Beyond that, the men were as much in the dark as their wives. "What do you think our chances are?" Karon would hound Ralph. "I don't know," he'd say. "But I'll do what I can to help." "Does it sound any good to you?" Joy would ask Gordon. "Sure," he'd reply. "I think it sounds great, if you think you can do it."

Karon and Joy had absolutely no doubts about their ability to handle virtually any nursing situation they might come up against. They had, after all, training and experience in almost every facet of the profession. Before transferring to psych, Joy had been in pediatrics, med/surg, and orthopedics, with occasional stints in the emergency room, obstetrics, and private-duty nursing. She'd dealt with patients recuperating from every conceivable type of surgery, suffering from myriad illnesses, coping with health problems that ranged from serious handicaps to temporary inconveniences. She had assisted with the very young and the very old, and she knew in her heart that she was good at her work.

So did Karon, whose first love had been the high-pressured, fast-moving job of the emergency room nurse. She too had seen the whole spectrum of patients—the heart attack victims, the kids with splinters in their feet, the teenaged gang members with bullet wounds in their backs, the overdose, the DOA, the hysterical, the comatose, the suicidal, and the insane. Between them the two women had seen the best and the worst of human nature and human ills. They knew how to cope because they'd been doing it for years. All they were doing now was enlarging the setting, from the hospital to the private office. Besides, they were only going to focus on blood pressures.

Still, they held back. By spring each had made the individual decision to go for the opportunity, but they hadn't committed themselves to each other. Each had some reservations about the other, each was second-guessing the other. Karon was sure Joy would have trouble coming up with her half of the incorporation money. She didn't want to push it. As for Joy, she thought Karon had more to give up, both in terms of her personal life-style and potentially, in terms of her job. Karon seemed reasonably content and Joy didn't want to ruin that.

They made their joint decision in April. Gordon had finally tired of hearing nothing but talk. One evening he asked Joy, "Why are you sitting on it? What are you waiting for?" She had no answer to give him. The next day, a Saturday, Joy was listening to the radio and heard a speaker say that if you couldn't invest in yourself, who could you invest in? That afternoon, she called her brother Jim and asked him to loan her $500. That night, at 1:00 A.M., she called Karon.

"Well, are we or aren't we? I'm ready."

Perhaps nothing was as disappointing to the women as the realization that *now* the hard part began. Making the decision was nothing next to actually establishing a business. They had to have a name before they could incorporate; they had to have an address before they could order stationery or a telephone; they had to know the size of their office before they could buy furniture; they had to have equipment and be set up before they could apply for malpractice insurance; they had to have insurance before they could open their doors. They needed a lab to send cultures and blood samples to; a medical consultant (John Castro, MD); an announcement for the local community paper and brochures for Joy's kids to pass out door to door, but before they could prepare these, they needed a logo. Karon had a friend whose husband was an artist, and he designed one for them. They liked it, a modification of the caduceus symbol with a twisted snake on one side and the profile of a woman on the other. She wore a nurse's cap, and the letters RN were discreetly tucked in the right-hand corner.

They also needed a bank account for the office. They had to find an accountant: how do you determine who is reliable when no one you know uses such a person? They had to find a lawyer. The Bar Association made recommendations and the man they finally selected, an expensive downtown attorney with splashy offices, treated them like a charity case. They didn't balk—they needed him, or so they thought. What about your husbands' names on the incorporation application? No, they said, this is ours, why should their names be on it? Karon and Joy didn't consider themselves liberated, just honest.

From May through August, Karon and Joy put themselves through a combined self-taught course on how to set up an independent nursing practice and how to open a business. Every free minute they were on the run. In June they rented an office, a small L-shaped room in a new, two-story brick building that hugged the inside corner of a small shopping center near the edge of the city. Orange draperies pulled across their front expanse of window and rust carpeting covered the floor. In July they began setting up. They added a white curtain to form a private space in the back, two used desks, a set of book shelves, one file cabinet, a set of white wrought-iron lawn furniture Ralph had found on sale. They ordered a sign and hung it in the door: "Registered Profes-

sional Nurses, Hours 10–1, Monday, Wednesday, and Friday."
Joy took care of buying supplies. Karon tried to get bank loans so
they'd have more operating capital, but was turned down.

With every phone call, the women learned. They began to
distinguish between the need to defer and the need to be assertive. They got over the shyness that plagues the uninitiated and
realized, eventually, it didn't matter if they asked dumb questions
as long as they got the information they needed They learned that
the world was not one uncomplicated piece of machinery, but a
honeycomb of individual compartments, each with its own code of
entry. Their calls demonstrated the importance of contacts; one
person would give them a lead to an organization or person they
never knew existed. At times the complications became dizzying;
then Karon realized the secret was not to take on the whole
problem at once, but rather to attack piece by piece. Most important, she realized that she, the individual, had to take the first
step, make the first inquiry, pick up the phone, and put through
the first tentative call. Otherwise, nothing would happen. They
were trying to penetrate a giant bureaucracy that never willingly
gave a piece of the action. If you wanted something done, you had
to do it yourself—no matter how difficult. Or terrifying.

The most elusive question facing Karon and Joy was one they
had to figure out for themselves: how much to charge. They
honestly had no idea, no criteria except that their fees had to be
less than those charged in a physician's office. They made up their
price list off the top of their heads, and although they insisted they
were going to do blood pressures only, they had the foresight to
make up fees for other services too, just in case. Blood pressure,
$3; diabetes test, $3; both for $5. Office visit, $5. Office visit with
injection, $5 plus the cost of the medication. Home visit with one
procedure, $10. Home visit for injection only, $10 plus the cost of
medication. Home visit with enema, $2 extra. Not once during
that summer did they sit down and seriously figure out how much
they had to earn each month to keep going. To them $400 sounded
reasonable, so that became their goal. They were groping, and
knew it, but didn't care.

All through August, while they waited for their malpractice policy to come through, Karon wrote letters. She borrowed a typewriter, pulled out her orange notebook, and made lists of people she thought should know about their practice. One letter was directed to physicians:

> Dear Doctor: The purpose of this letter is to
> inform you of a new service available to you for
> the care of your patients.
>
> Recently, Registered Nurses have begun to practice
> the profession on a self-employed office basis in
> order that good professional nursing care not be
> restricted only to the critically or terminally ill
> in the hospital. Our corporation. . . .

Another was composed for business and professional organizations. Karon must have sent a hundred letters offering to do blood pressures, physical exams, and other employee testing. Most firms replied with polite refusals, a few offered words of encouragement, but none were ready to commit themselves to the untried and unproven services of Registered Professional Nurses, PC. Karon was undaunted; she wrote even more letters; she coerced her partner into helping.

*   *   *   *   *

On Monday morning, September 11, 1973, Joy Catterson walked out her front door, down a 12-foot stretch of narrow concrete and out onto the quiet, deserted sidewalk on her dead-end street. The Little League park on the corner was empty and only a few cars were parked along the curb. Still, Joy felt as if the world were watching her, taking bets, laying the odds. She was nervous. The malpractice insurance policy had arrived in the mail just a few days earlier. There was no turning back now. The business was a reality. It was waiting for her.

Beneath all Joy's concerns that morning lay her real worry: would she see her children often enough, have enough time for them? The girls were in school, but the boys. . . . She held one by each hand, the four-year-old eager and pulling and the two-year-old still clumsily propelling himself along on feet that wouldn't move as fast as the rest of his body.

Joy had thought the large 2-by-3-foot sign on the driver's side of her car (Registered Professional Nurses: 222-3819) would embarrass her. Instead, she looked at it proudly and gave it a quick pat, almost of affection, as she would her children when they came to her for help or praise. But she was blushing as she moved out of the residential streets and onto the main thoroughfare, driving the boys to the babysitter she'd lined up. Before, her hours had always meshed with Gordon's and he had watched the children while she worked; now that would change. Would the boys like the babysitter? Would she have time to get back home on the days she had to car pool the girls to and from school? The business she wasn't worried about; her family, she was. Those thoughts kept her almost too busy to notice that, yes, people were looking.

That same morning, Karon White Gibson—she'd started including her maiden name almost unconsciously—got into her car miles away. Her's had the same sign as Joy's attached to the driver's door, but when Karon looked at it, all she could hope was that it didn't look out of place on her car. After all, she thought, people expected doctors to drive Cadillacs, but not nurses. Karon was as excited about their venture as Joy was apprehensive. She knew she'd miss her old life—ten o'clock alarm; two or three cigarettes, coffee, and the morning paper; a few laps in the pool; an hour in the sun; just generally taking it easy in the hours before work began at the hospital. But would she regret tossing it away? No more eight-hour days and late parties. Now they'd be more like 14 hours and no parties. But that's what she'd wanted, wasn't it? And now if it was going to succeed she'd have to work at it. Yet, as much as her imagination might want to believe otherwise, Karon knew she and Joy had no guarantees. She knew that all their drive, dedication, and ability meant nothing, that the world was a cruel and often arbitrary judge of who made it and who didn't.

She and Joy were, in a sense, like two kids opening up a lemonade stand on the corner during a hot summer spell. She'd seen it happen too many times: the card table, the pitcher, the sign, and two eager faces smiling out innocently at the world for hours until finally, confused and hurt, they drink the lemonade no one else wanted. (But it seemed like such a good idea; everyone gets thirsty when it's hot.) And they trudge home with their empty cash box. (We're not charging much, honest!) And their broken dream. (Nobody came, everyone thought it was just a game.)

Karon and Joy meant business. Now they had to prove it. As Karon drove along she tried to ignore the fears of being sued, tried to forget the pharmacist's prediction that their parking lot would be filled with lawyers from the AMA, tried not to worry about how they'd pay the bills, and desperately tried to focus on one problem—the one she was convinced was the key to success: how to let the world know what they were doing. Nobody's ever even heard of us, she thought. Nobody knows we're here.

Karon and Joy were in business, the first nurses in the Midwest to establish a corporate practice on their own. Registered Professional Nurses, PC. Karon White Gibson, RN, President. Joy Smith Catterson, RN, Vice President.

They were so immensely proud that first official day. They sat in their pretty little office, waiting, just waiting. They had spent nearly all of the $1,000 they'd had in the bank to start with. They had only fifty dollars left. They waited. The telephone rang once. A social worker had seen their announcement and asked them to make a home visit to an elderly woman. "Yes, sure." Joy was ecstatic. She would make the visit the next day. Three hours later, the phone rang again. Forget it, the social worker said, the patient had just died.

At two o'clock Karon and Joy locked the door, got into their cars, and drove to their regular jobs at General. They were ready to break the news. They hoped everyone would be excited and happy for them. But the other nurses were angry and jealous. Why hadn't Joy and Karon included them? Why hadn't they thought of the idea first? They wished the two luck, but coldly. Karon tried to call the Director of Nursing and overheard the woman tell her secretary: "If she has anything to say, she should tell it to her supervisor." Later, the director called Karon back and congratulated her. "Talk about the business all you want. I checked with PR and they said it's fine for you to say you work here, but please no other mention of the hospital." The director also said she hoped neither Karon nor Joy would decide to leave their jobs at the hospital—"but if you do, just give us a month's notice." Karon assured her she had no intention of ever leaving General.

On the second day at their independent practitioner's office, Karon and Joy got one more phone call. On the third day, a series of people called, all asking about home visits. The blood pressure manometers hadn't been touched. Guess we were wrong, the nurses said, guess if we're going to make it we'll have to do everything. The first two weeks in business confirmed their suspicion. As word of the nurses' practice got around, Karon and Joy were called upon for a variety of services. Legally, they could not prescribe medications or diagnose illness, but beyond that they were free to do everything nurses do in hospitals or in doctors' offices. The old dream of block-long lines of people with shirt sleeves rolled up waiting for a blood pressure measurement had been a fantasy. For the first time, Karon and Joy realized this was no small thing they'd gotten themselves into.

chapter six

Addison Clark was the first patient to walk through the doors of Registered Professional Nurses, PC. He was tall, in his late thirties, slender, with dark bushy hair and a casual, slightly unkempt appearance. Despite a smiling, eager face, he seemed hesitant, almost apologetic, as he stepped lightly across the rust carpet. If he had worn a hat he probably would have held it nervously in his hands, twirling the brim through his fingers like a young James Stewart.

But he didn't have a hat. Instead, clutched in his right hand was a doctor's order for treatment.

"Here," he said smiling. "I guess I have to give this to you."

So this is the guy who phoned yesterday, Karon thought, glancing at the sheet. She remembered taking a call from a man who said he was constipated from being on a diet and needed an enema. "We'll need a doctor's order," Karon had told him, hoping to divert the man to his own physician. Obviously, the tactic hadn't worked. Now Karon turned and handed the slip of paper to her partner; enemas were Joy's department.

Karon began her questioning. Addison Clark was, they learned, 39 years old, married, the father of two children, a government computer operator who worked nights and whose only hobby was photography. When Joy asked what kind of pictures Clark took, he replied they were the "interesting" kind and winked. Joy kicked Karon under the desk. As for medical history, Addison Clark had had a problem with headaches for a while, had his appendix removed as a teenager, no allergies, no ongoing problems. He'd had difficulty with his left foot once, pain in the arch, but he'd been to a podiatrist for that. It was fine now. Once he'd had an outbreak of blackheads in the groin area (gross, thought Karon, I'm going to be ill), but a woman doctor had fixed that. The kids used to pick on him when he was a child and he was raised by his old aunt, who gave him daily enemas until he was a teenager. No, he wasn't currently seeing a psychiatrist. He'd been to one but the medicine he was supposed to take made him lose control of his bladder and he didn't like that, so he stopped. What was the psychiatrist's name? Clark didn't remember. Would he find out, for their records? Sure. After the questions, it was on the scale, then back to Joy for a blood pressure reading, and finally the visit was over.

When Clark left, reassured that Karon would call that evening or the next morning with his enema schedule, he waved from the door as a little boy would when leaving his grandmother's house, his face all in a grin. "My teeth hurt sometimes," he said, as if joking, "from smiling so much."

"Don't worry." It was a direct order from Karon. The first words spoken after the door slammed shut and the two nurses relaxed from their professional, dismiss-the-patient stance.

"Don't worry! Who does he think he's kidding? Karon, I'm the one who has to be alone with this guy in that rest room and you're saying don't worry. He's borderline, and that's being generous. You see all those nervous twitches? Did you pick up on all those hints? He meant that about his teeth. I don't like it, not one bit, but I know I'm going to do it."

Karon made herself laugh. She became flip and accused Joy of having been a psych nurse too long. "You're seeing things that aren't there; besides, I'll check with his doctor. She'll know him," she said, but what she really meant was that they had to take chances. They'd already taken the big one, so what difference did the little ones make now? "We'll think of something." Karon had handled worse patients than this before in the psych ward. Addison Clark didn't scare her.

That afternoon Ralph came to pick up Karon and they told him about their problem. "Just have someone hiding in the little closet back there with the hot water heater," he suggested. "I'll take the day off and do it if you want."

"That's stupid," Karon said. "Why should you take a day off?" Instead, they nominated Gordon for the job. He had the day off.

The men's room was small, with one stall along the south wall and a sink opposite. Behind these, on the back wall was a narrow louvered door that hid a small crawl space, the spot where the hot water heater stood. When Joy went to inspect the room, she jiggled the interior door open and peered inside. The heater closet was dark and cramped, stuffy too, but Joy crawled in, stooped down, and tried to look out the door. You couldn't see between the slats but you certainly could hear anything that went on in the bathroom.

A minute later Joy strode past Karon. "Hold on, I'll be right back." And she was, coming out of their office with a small stool which she took into the men's room. When Joy reappeared her hands were empty. She talked, as she led Karon back through their door.

"Gordon is going to be in there sitting on that stool in that little cubby hole behind the louvered door—just like the one in the ladies' room—next to the water heater, with his gun on and ready to rescue me if Addison Clark gets smart."

"Well, I'll be standing in the hall with a can of MACE too, in case anything happens," Karon said.

"That's fine, Karon. But Gordon is still going to be in there with me. Okay? Is that settled?" It was.

After his first and only enema, Addison Clark became a regular patient. He came mainly to talk; he said he trusted them and needed someone to talk to. Slowly, the story of a sad, tortured soul unwound before them. Clark had many fears. Fear of crossing a bridge, even in a car; fear of being underground; fear his wife might get pregnant and worse fear because she could not. Karon and Joy sent him to a urologist for a sperm count, which turned out to be normal; they kept urging him to go to a doctor for his high blood pressure, which he refused to do; but mostly the two women listened.

Clark talked about white lights that flashed before his eyes, about needing to drive fast because he felt more in control then, about hating sharp objects and not wanting them anywhere near. At one point he insisted on coming to see Karon and Joy more often and they refused—too busy, too expensive for him. Actually, they were worried about cultivating the patient's dependency on them. As it was, he already phoned them several times each day their business was open. One day Clark left their office and walked to his car, which was parked near their door. For two hours he lay on the front seat, maybe sleeping, maybe watching them. Someone in the building called the police and when the squad arrived the officer sauntered over looking friendly but concerned. "Son," he said, "we don't want to see this car in this lot again." The next day, in the driving rain, Addison Clark arrived on a bicycle. He wore a dark brown slicker and sat outside for an hour before pedaling away.

Gently, Karon and Joy urged the unhappy man to seek psychiatric care. "No," he insisted. "You do better. Besides, if the psychiatrist hurts himself falling out of his chair, I'll be blamed because we're alone in his office."

For Christmas, Clark brought them a box of Fannie May candy and a book of McDonald's gift certificates. For the new year he brought them his secret; he had something within himself, something that happened ten years before, that he couldn't tell anyone, not even them. Joy was convinced he'd killed someone. Karon didn't believe that, even though once, while he was babysitting for some friends, Clark had called saying he was afraid he would cut their baby into tiny little pieces.

"No, you won't," Karon had said. "You're going to talk to me instead."

For an hour she stayed on the phone, torn between her obligation to the patient and the confidential nature of their relationship and an intense desire to call the police and have them check on

Clark, make sure he hadn't already harmed the child—if, in fact, there really was a baby involved. Finally, Clark seemed to have calmed down. Over the phone Karon heard a doorbell ring. The parents had come for the child, she could let Clark go at last.

By now, Addison Clark's appointments were scheduled only for Wednesdays. That was Ralph's day off, and during the time Clark sat downstairs talking to the two nurses, Ralph sat upstairs in an empty office, working on some of the nurses' books and waiting for a scream or some commotion. But nothing ever happened.

Then one day, a dark gloomy morning, when Clark was feeling unusually morose and quite talkative, he told them about the dream he'd had.

"It's one of those that keeps coming back, over and over. I see a lady in it, a pretty lady, and in the dream I rape her. I slap her around and push her down. Then I push myself over her and I have a huge erection. It's wonderful." Even as he talked, Clark's mood swung from high to low; he was animated and excited, then subdued and mumbling to the floor. On one of his swings down, Karon and Joy looked searchingly at each other over his bowed head. Their faces mirrored each other, pale and set.

"Anybody we know?" Joy asked.

"Yes." Clark seemed surprised at the question, as if he assumed everyone knew. His head came up then and he looked directly across the desk to where Joy was sitting, not two feet away. "It's you, nurse."

On the surface, Joy didn't react at all. She sat unmoving in her chair. Inside, however, she sensed a violent tremor, just the whisper of a shaking, horrid fear that when it surfaced it would contort her entire body and make her physically ill. She was terrified. She had been raped by Clark's words if not by his actions and now, like a true victim, she felt vulnerable and helpless.

From then on Joy refused to be present when Addison Clark came for an appointment. Karon sat alone listening to Clark hinting of suicide, of being told by the voices that he should kill himself. Clark spoke in his usual singsong voice, lilting up, then gloomily coming down. He sounded at times like a four-year-old having a serious discussion on life with a teddy bear. Suddenly, one day the voice changed and Karon caught herself grabbing the arms of her chair. She'd only witnessed this kind of thing once before. It was eerie, fascinating and revolting at the same time. Clark's other voice was not intelligible but it was clearly a distinct, different voice emanating through his lips, grasping for an entry to the world, then losing hold and slipping back into the netherland of his mind. Clark didn't realize anything unusual had happened, of course; he was talking about his job now, saying he'd actually come to enjoy it and liked the hours and the people. Then he left.

Karon called Joy immediately. They decided they had to force Clark to seek psychiatric care, no more urging or advising. They had only one weapon, his dependence on them, and they would use it. Karon told him the following week: "No more appointments with us unless you are also seeing a psychiatrist." Clark balked and whined. He went away and didn't call for two weeks. When he came back, Karon refused him an appointment because he hadn't seen a doctor yet. "Okay," he finally agreed, "but I'll go only if he lets me come here too. I don't want to leave you. I need you." So Clark, now under psychiatric care, continued to visit the nurses.

Other people needed them as well. One day, Karon came to the office to find a series of messages from a Mrs. Grotson who lived in a nearby suburb. When Karon finally reached her, Mrs. Grotson explained that her husband, Joe, had been hospitalized several months earlier with what the VA medical doctors said was a virus and the VA psychiatrist said was a psychosis. Whatever the cause, Mr. Grotson, a gentle-looking man in his mid-fifties, suffered a paralysis extending into the upper extremities and the urinary tract. He was bedridden and unable to perform normal bodily functions except with the aid of a urinary catheter. After treating him in the hospital for nearly six weeks—with no change in his condition—the doctors sent him home, strapped to a ferris-wheel-like Striker bed and equipped with supplementary urinary equipment. Someone at the hospital, Mrs. Grotson could never remember just who, explained that a family member could be taught to irrigate and to change the catheter. Because Mrs. Grotson suffered slight palsy, she was ruled out. Instead, the mysterious someone at the hospital decided the daughter—a 16-year-old high school junior—should be taught the procedures and even went so far as to arrange for the girl to be on a work study program at school so she'd be home four hours each day to attend her father.

The girl was hysterical. She'd completed the hospital's one-hour training session but could not bring herself to face her father. He too was embarrassed and lay like a museum exhibit on his outsize bed with pain shooting through his body, and his face turned to the wall. Mrs. Grotson told Karon and Joy how she'd pleaded with her daughter and tried to reason with her husband, admitting in the next breath she was as repulsed as they. Then she'd tried the local Visiting Nurses Association. They'd sent a nurse out, but she wouldn't deal with the catheter.

"You know what I finally had to do?" Mrs. Grotson went on. "That thing had to be changed, so Sherri and me and the neighbor put Joe in a sleeping bag we borrowed and we carried him out to the car. We got an old station wagon and we lay him out gentle as we could in the back with the seats down and all and we go to the emergency room. That poor man, we tried to drive easy, but you know how it is. Medicaid said they wouldn't pay for it because he was an outpatient. Cost me seventy-five dollars each time. I can't afford it but I have no choice. Three times we did that. Then someone told me about you. Will you change that thing?"

Mrs. Grotson sat with her hands jumping lightly in her lap. Her face, ashen, twitched periodically and even her overweight body seemed to move involuntarily in its old red chair. She was a beaten woman. Looking forlorn and desperate in the heavy silence that followed her soliloquy, Mrs. Grotson absently chewed at her lower lip.

Only peripherally were the women aware of soft noises coming from the kitchen; then they caught quick glimpses of a skinny girl in blue jeans and tee shirt moving self-consciously across the doorway. "That's Sherri," Mrs. Grotson whispered, picking up on Joy and Karon's glances. "I can't really fault her. She tried so hard to help her daddy, but to do that!" And the thought trailed off because it was simply too hard to face again.

In the bedroom Karon and Joy squeezed past each other in the narrow space left by the huge bed as they talked rather boisterously to their patient. They'd asked Sherri to make a cup of tea for her mother, then gave orders they were not to be disturbed. They would change the catheter on Joe's doctor's orders and perform any other nursing service necessary. Cheerfully yet. Heaven only knew how much these people could stand a little cheer.

After a few months the Grotsons were like old friends. Sherri was back in school on a regular schedule again and Karon and Joy rarely saw her, but Mrs. Grotson would have a pot of coffee on for them, and the two nurses would sit and chat a bit with her after finishing with Joe. He had tried to thank them once but the words had caught somewhere between his heart and his lips. They knew what he meant and he knew they did, so everything was fine. Registered Professional Nurses charged $15 for each visit and Mrs. Grotson happily paid.

Once when Mr. Grotson began to hemorrhage Karon called Dr. Castro (Joe's personal physician was willing to order antibiotic treatment over the phone, but he balked at a home visit). When John waltzed in full of aplomb and concern, he waved away Mrs. Grotson's apologies for her home and acted for all the world as if he were treating his personal and most favored patient. It was obvious Mrs. Grotson was concerned about the bill she would receive from him; she could hardly believe it when Dr. Castro charged her only $25.

Eventually, Joe Grotson was given an external catheter, and didn't require the nurses' services anymore. As seemed their fate, they moved on. Their next home patient was a woman crippled by arthritis. When Karon and Joy first saw her, Adrienne Snelly lay shriveled in a crumpled old bed, a bowl full of pills within easy reach on the nightstand. Through the glass sides of the dish one could see a half-dozen different colors, sizes, and shapes of capsules and tablets; there were at least 400 pieces of medication in the container.

The woman could do nothing but dial her bedside telephone with a pencil. She suffered from an infected hip wound, hadn't sat on a toilet or had a bath for seven years. Since the illness had crippled her, Adrienne had been a prisoner of her bed, except for an occasional push in a wheelchair into the living room or kitchen when her husband or daughter felt a need to change her location. Now that the daughter had moved out, the woman was terrified. A neighbor came in three times a day to check on her and give her a bedpan, but having the neighbor help out meant leaving the front door unlocked all day, while Adrienne lay helpless in her room. (Why the husband wouldn't give the neighbor a key no one would say.)

When Karon and Joy called the woman's doctor and told him about the draining infection, he ordered a special solution that had been popular during World War II but was no longer commercially available. Never mind, they found a pharmacist who would mix the ingredients, so they could make up the solution and irrigate the wound on every visit. They also got the woman into the tub, a major undertaking that required removing the sliding glass shower doors, then maneuvering the old lady into the wheelchair, across the hall, out of the wheelchair, and into a bathroom built for one body, not three. Karon, who had previously injured an arm, always took the feet while Joy, petite by any standard, but especially tiny next to her partner, hauled the heavier upper portion of the torso. Save for one incident when Joy backed into the space heater set up in the bathroom and Karon nearly slipped on a wet floor, the baths were a cinch.

Adrienne Snelly was their patient for only one month, but in that time she blossomed. The baths relaxed her, the passive exercises the nurses administered helped loosen the patient's joints, and the visits in general helped to give the woman a psychological boost. For the first time in years, Adrienne had a little excitement in her life. When a local news crew called Registered Professional Nurses and said they wanted to film the nurses doing a home visit, Karon suggested using Adrienne as the subject. "We'll want to film your arrival," the TV man said, "so make sure you show up after we do."

On the day of the shoot, Joy and Karon sent one of their associate nurses to help Adrienne prepare for the event. She put on her best housedress and sat with hair combed and makeup on, ready for her TV debut. She was inside fretting over her appearance while outside Karon and Joy raced around one-way streets trying to get their car pointed in the right direction for the cameras.

"Just remember to relax," Karon said, as they made their final approach.

Somehow, they did it—got to the front door, into the living room, and onto the couch where they sat on either side of a beaming Adrienne, all the while pretending to ignore the cameras that dominated the landscape. Karon and Joy talked about home care, about house calls, and about their services for patients like Mrs. Snelly.

"What about hospital costs, all this we hear about the high cost of hospital care?" the reporter asked Karon.

"Is that thing on?" she asked, pointing to the tape recorder.

"No."

But Karon could hear the quiet clicking of the rotating tape. They're not going to fool me, she thought. If I say anything against hospitals, General will have my scalp. So she went on telling about all the "hidden" costs hospitals have, explaining reasons for not criticizing the escalating cost of hospital care.

The television debut brought more business to Karon and Joy and provided a psychological boost. It helped Adrienne as well. One week after the shoot, on a frosty November day, the patient announced that she wanted to go outside, something she hadn't done in five years. "I'd like to visit my neighbor," she said, so Karon and Joy bundled Adrienne into her wheelchair, then carried her and the chair down the front stairs, pushed her across the sidewalk, carried her up the neighbor's steps, rang the doorbell, and ran to hide behind two bushes. When the neighbor opened the door, Adrienne held her arms out for a hug and cried.

Later she even wanted to attend a wedding the family had been invited to. But despite the nurses' urging, Adrienne's husband refused to take her. "I can't cope with that thing," he said, meaning the wheelchair. And he said no again when Karon and Joy offered to take care of transporting his wife to the reception. He wouldn't be able to deal with it, he said.

It seemed there was much he couldn't cope with. When Karon and Joy arranged for Meals on Wheels for Adrienne, he told his wife to cancel it. When they encouraged her to call friends more often, he complained about the cost. One day, with shocking directness, he spoke to Karon, "Is there anything you can do to speed up the process?" he asked. "You know, help her out of her misery sooner."

Eventually, Adrienne had to be hospitalized because of a problem with her hip. From a taste of freedom, from three glorious baths a week, from specialized treatment with the pink solution, Adrienne went to a modern adult cradle, a basin of wash water, and a bedpan. She was to have her hip pinned. She never made it. Adrienne Snelly died in a hospital bed, alone and foresaken. Her husband remarried in three months, still arguing over the last bill RPN had sent him (80 percent of which was reimbursed by his private insurance carrier).

Sometimes the juxtaposition of their patients was painfully ironic. One morning Karon and Joy went to the 11-room apartment of a couple who recently won one million dollars in the Illinois state lottery. The nurses performed life insurance physicals on both the husband and the wife, chatted eagerly about the good fortune of instant, painless wealth, and enjoyed the moment

99

of panic caused when Karon slipped on a patch of ice going down the front stairs. "Oh, God, can I pick the place to fall! If I were to hurt myself this would be the place to do it." On the afternoon of the same day, the nurse practitioners visited three elderly, impoverished sisters who lived in a tiny frame structure with a shaky front porch and paint peeling on the inside walls. The youngest sister, who was 64, worked at a clerical job and was the sole support of the other two: Agnes, who'd had her leg amputated as a child and had never gotten a prosthesis, and Clara, victim of a degenerative nerve disease that had left her bedridden since 1946.

At one end of town, the nurses cared for a wispy old woman they affectionately referred to as "Motha." Motha lived in near splendor, occupying her own small wing in her daughter's rambling, antique-filled home. "Oh, do be careful with Motha," the daughter, herself about 50, would say every time Karon and Joy lifted the patient to the tub. "Oh, I'm afraid Motha seems to have soiled herself," the daughter would sometimes report just as they were putting their coats on to leave. "You'll have to wash her again." Motha suffered from a touch of senility. She'd been a pianist once, and a grand piano sat unused in her sitting room, while Motha sat every day in her boudoir wrapped in layers of delicate lace underwear and bed clothes that had to be carefully pinned and arranged around her shrinking body. Joy and Karon imagined her a beautiful young woman living in a world of politeness and niceties, whirling around ballroom floors in long chintz dresses, with the same ribbons and bows running through them as graced the edges of her old lady, confined-in-bed attire.

At the other edge of the community lived Gladys, a real Tugboat Annie, who'd been pelted by a series of life's injustices. Gladys raged against them all. She had six children who never came to visit ("the little bastards"); an alcoholic husband whom she fought with constantly ("He brings men here to make it with me!"); and a mysterious, crippling pain in her left leg that made it almost impossible for her to walk ("Ain't that a bitch, a game leg").

As best as she could, Gladys, 58, roamed around in a filthy house filled with food crumbs and overturned plants. She could not be treated gently. She screamed at Karon and Joy just as she screamed at life, but they came right back at her. Together, they wrestled the obese, kicking form into the bathroom, sat her on a chair in the tub, and turned the shower on, literally hosing down her greasy body. Gladys and Karon and Joy worked out a fine, stand-off relationship until the patient's husband and kids got together for once and managed to run the old woman into a nursing home. Karon and Joy missed Gladys, but soon they took on one of their most poignant cases.

The call came in about two days after a local paper ran a photo of the independent practitioners, showing them on a home visit. The discharge nurse at a local hospital read the story and wanted to know if they could handle one of the hospital's patients who was being released the next day. The nurse said she'd already called the Visiting Nurses Association but was told the case was too complicated for the agency to handle. Registered Professional Nurses agreed to take it on, and that afternoon Karon and Joy went to the hospital to observe the particular technique that was required for the patient. There they met Rita Coines.

The patient said she was 47; she looked 80. She could take nothing by mouth, only a few sips of water or an ice chip, and could move only slowly and with great difficulty. From under her covers ran a long familiar line of plastic, a gastro tube feeder, and a second, thinner line, a subclavean IV. This was inserted not in the arm or hand but was imbedded deep into the flesh of the chest near the heart. "They tried to teach my daughter how to operate it, gave her a complete lesson in less than an hour. Can you imagine, all this fancy treatment and all this expensive stuff they've got and they try to teach a 22-year-old secretary to cope with one of these things? I don't even trust her to sew a button on." Rita's eyes begged Karon and Joy to laugh at her joke, but the nurses couldn't. They could do nothing but stare at the pain that was so powerful it seemed to radiate from the woman's skin.

Neither Karon nor Joy had studied subclavean IVs in school and now they watched as the hospital staff demonstrated the procedure for changing the dressing around the sterile area. That's all they had to do, they were told; they were not to change the needle itself. What's so complicated about that? Karon thought. It's just a sterile dressing change. She and Joy agreed thev'd be able to handle the patient on their own. The woman was sent home that afternoon and from then on the nurses saw her there on a regular basis.

Rita Coines was a bloated, waxen figure suffering from cancer. She told Karon and Joy how her stomach had suddenly swelled up one day after she'd felt a sharp pain in her leg. She'd gone to one of the area teaching and research hospitals, because "I'd heard it was the best." There, Rita Coines was diagnosed as having widespread cancer that the doctors felt was treatable but would require heroic measures. "They asked me to be a research patient, that I'd get the best and newest treatment and I wouldn't have to pay. Well, we didn't have very good insurance and I was just so afraid of all those bills and then having to sell the house to pay, so I said yes."

It was an effort for the woman to talk but she insisted and seemed almost pleased to have to do it. Mrs. Coines told the nurses about her surgeries, the first to remove a malignant breast, then the others, the exploratory procedures that left her feeling weaker each time. She'd had chemotherapy treatments too and radiation and she didn't know what all. No, she'd never had her own personal doctor, "never needed one before." In the hospital Mrs. Coines simply accepted whatever happened to her. She asked what questions she could and took whatever answers were given. "I knew I was dying," she said. "I knew it long before anyone told me. When they said it, finally, one of the doctors had come in. He apologized almost and said they'd tried everything. I wasn't angry with him, he seemed so helpless. But the next day one of the social service people came and said I'd either have to pay for my treatment from then on or leave." Rita Coines' voice barely broke when she told how she had come home with four months to live.

Three times a week for three months Karon and Joy visited the quiet unpretentious house. Once they had to call in Dr. Castro when the tube feeder was blocked, and they sat with Rita the two hours it took before he could get there. Once they came to find Mrs. Coines had been to the hospital the day before for a scheduled check on the tube. "And those bastards didn't even change the dressing," she told Karon and Joy. "They just taped the old one back on."

Rarely in their visits did the nurses see Neil, Rita's husband, but they learned through snatches of conversation that he and Rita had been on the outs for some time. Now he avoided the house as much as possible, leaving early in the morning and returning late in the evening. He'd fixed a place to sleep in the basement and stayed there when he was in. Rita's one consolation upon leaving the hospital was that she would have time to change her will so it excluded Neil entirely. "I haven't much to leave anyone," she said, "but he'll get nothing. He's already had the better part of my life."

Everything Rita owned would go to her ten-year-old son and her daugher. Her daughter was an attractive young woman, tall and slender with deep green eyes and short brown hair, dark-complected and serious, like a study for a painting. But she looked haunted and she was, by the specter of her mother's disfigurement, by the sure knowledge of her death. "You tell her to go out, have fun; she won't listen to me," Rita told the nurses, so they did. Alone in the kitchen they sat with Carol and asked about boyfriends and dates; she shyly admitted she didn't have any. "I don't have time. I can't leave her." Partly to make Rita feel better and partly because they felt sorry for the young woman, Joy and Karon convinced Bill, their telephone installation man, to agree to a blind date. A perfect match, they were convinced. The next week they learned the date had lasted one hour. All Carol had wanted to do, Bill said, was drive by the nurses' office. She insisted on seeing what it looked like. Then she made Bill take her home. She was torn by guilt, insisting she had to get back and look after her mother.

Carol was honest with Karon and Joy: she had no idea how she would face her mother's death. "You should have known her. She wasn't the woman you see lying there helpless. She was a beautiful woman, you know, a live wire, the real life of the party. I remember her singing to me when I was little, and all the time I was growing up I remember her laughing and telling jokes. Did you know she used to be a WAC?" And Carol brought out the picture of a tall, thin, proud young woman who held her head high and looked out at life with eager beautiful eyes "That's the mother I remember." Carol said looking at them with her sad, steady face. "I owe her something, I owe her everything. That's why I can't leave her. Going to work is bad enough; all day I'm gone. The rest of the time I just have to be here."

Karon was dying for a cigarette—she saw them in her purse when she reached for a notebook. There was something she wanted to write down. She put the thought of a smoke out of her head.

"Did your mother have a social worker on her case at the hospital?"

"Sure," Carol said, her gaze indicating she thought the question rather odd.

"And it's on your mother's records that she was a WAC?"

Carol nodded.

"They never told you or your mother she was eligible for free treatment and other benefits at the veterans' hospital?"

The young woman shook her head slowly, she was thinking, reaching back into her memory. "No," she said finally. "No—not ever." They'd thought of it themselves once, but only briefly. To them the VA hospital was a big sign that said MEN ONLY. Carol couldn't believe that women were treated there also "I'll look into it, but don't tell mother." she pleaded "It would break her heart."

But it was too late. Although Rita would experience no major crisis, she never got better; each day she simply grew a little worse. And then one day, in her daughter's arms, with Carol's tears dropping on her coarse gray hair and the young woman's soft soothing words of lullaby singing gently in her ears, Rita Coines complained of feeling cold and of falling. Then she died.

If Neil mourned the passing of his wife, no one ever knew. Carol did, greatly. So too did Joy and Karon, who felt they'd lost a friend.

chapter seven

*D*uring the first five months of their practice, Joy and Karon were featured twice on television news shows and were written up three times in area newspapers. The publicity made them celebrities. People recognized them on the street: "Aren't you the nurses we saw on TV?" they'd ask, or "Good luck!" they'd say. Shortly after one broadcast, Karon and Joy visited their lawyer. The man, who'd rather scorned them before, greeted them personally in his waiting area and offered coffee, asking their pardon of a few minutes' delay while he "tied up some loose ends." He even delivered a portable phone to them in the waiting room.

The limelight embarrassed Joy but it fed Karon's ego. All her life she'd read about newsmakers and wondered who were these people in the headlines. Now she knew. They were people with something new, something unique, possibly helpful, to offer, like the two of them. Karon's message was simple: to potential patients she talked about saving money on medical visits for basic maintenance care and about convenience and professionalism on home visits. To other nurses she carried a subtle message of, "Look what we can do if we try." To the world in general it was, "Hey! The ladies aren't so dumb after all."

Nursing had been the common element that brought Joy and Karon together. The independent practice bound them even closer, making their lives more and more similar and totally different from what they'd been before. Joy and Karon had become businesswomen. This new identity overshadowed their existence. Karon no longer had time for a heavy social schedule;

Joy no longer was able to think of herself as simply mother and housewife. They both had the something more they'd been looking for and it affected the very core of their lives.

Joy and Karon thought differently now; they acted differently too. Before, for example, if they were going to attend a police wives' auxiliary dinner, they'd talk about what they should wear and what the menu would be. Now, they'd ask themselves who they were going to meet and what they could talk about that would help the business. When they saw pictures of themselves splashed across newspaper feature sections, they evaluated their hairstyles and hem lines not on the basis of fashion but on the basis of image and whether the look they were projecting would help or hurt the business.

The two had become virtually inseparable. In addition to working together at the hospital and in their practice, they spoke to senior citizen's groups, attended nursing conferences, and talked to community organizations—all to draw attention to the services their business offered. Sometimes, because of her family, Joy had a more complicated time scheduling herself between the hospital and the practice and Karon would have to help out by babysitting. "Buy me a Coke," Joy's oldest boy once demanded of Karon, who was waiting with him and his younger brother while Joy was undergoing a breast exam and pap smear.

"No." Karon believed in being firm. Suddenly the boy jumped up, turned accusingly to her, and in a loud, pitiful voice sobbed, "Mommy, you haven't fed me in three days and now you won't even give me a Coke." Lord, thought Karon, busy hustling the two boys out of the door and out of ear range of the half-dozen other women in the waiting room, this is what it means to have children. How does Joy do it? While Karon mused, the boys prepared to sprint off. She lurched at them just in time and grabbed both by their collars, but the kids were faster than Karon anticipated and smarter too. They simply slipped out of the jacket sleeves and ran off leaving a frustrated Karon standing like a human clothes rack.

Joy waved away her friend's consternation. "They do that all the time," she said. "Well, you've certainly got more patience than I do," Karon mumbled during the ride home. "You mean you've only just discovered that?" Joy said, laughing at her partner. Only later did Joy realize this was the first time she'd been the least cavalier with Karon. She liked the feeling.

More and more, Joy was flexing her muscles and losing some of her previous shyness. (She remembered one day for no reason that at the twentieth reunion of her high school class only two people had known who she was, as if she'd never been at the same school with the other 400 people in the room.) Joy wasn't sure what prompted her next move, the constant reruns of *Emergency* on television that her children often watched or just the talks with Karon about how medicine was changing and how men were moving into a variety of newly created and better paying jobs. Whatever it was, Joy decided to look into becoming a paramedic. Why not? she thought. Nurses conduct many of the courses. I probably know all the stuff already. Why should all the paramedics be men?

"Sorry," the nasal voice on the other end of the phone whined. "You're not qualified. You have to take the course."

"But I'm a registered nurse and nurses teach the courses," Joy argued.

"You want to teach a course here, fine. You want to take the trainees out on mock runs, fine. But you can't be a paramedic. You're not eligible. Besides you don't want to sleep with them, and smell their dirty feet."

"What other benefits do you have?" Joy asked, and the woman hung up.

Joy was angry. She wasn't going to go to school to study what she already knew. That would be belittling. Later Karon heard of a Chicago area RN who had actually completed the paramedic's course, not very happily either. "The whole time they were in training, she wasn't allowed to touch a patient!" Karon was so mad she nearly shouted at Joy as they drove from one home visit to another. "Only the senior paramedic could physically touch the patients, and this woman had been a nurse for 20 years! Do you know what they told her, why these guys think they're so much better than nurses? Because they do auto excavation. 'We have to carry patients, and nurses couldn't do that.' Who do they think carried patients before paramedics were invented? If I had a dollar for every patient I ever carried, I could practically retire now."

At their office Karon and Joy were learning to enjoy the camaraderie of the other business people in the building. The travel agent down the hall, a woman, was delighted to see them settle in. In no time they were answering each other's phones; the nurses took her blood pressure free and she offered them discounts on travel. "Bring me business and I'll reciprocate." The buddy system at work. Karon and Joy marvelled at it. The pharmacist, a friendly middle-aged man, who'd tried to discourage them initially, finally came around. His only problem was his odd sense of humor. One day he strode in the front door to casually announce that a small plane had crashed nearby, narrowly missing a police squad car. "What the hell," he said. "Who'd miss a couple of cops? The world would be better off without them anyway." Karon shoved him outside and slammed the door in his face for that one.

Upstairs from Registered Professional Nurses was an insurance office. The agent didn't like Karon's independent ways—he called her a 'black widow'—but he had his eye on Joy.

Poor Joy. No one ever believed she was the older, that she had four children. She just looked too innocent, too nice. And every time Joy asked to use the agent's copying machine, he'd find himself with a bad case of the roving hands. He too had a poor sense of humor. "You'd be better off running a house of prostitution. It's more lucrative; yeah, you should be prostitutes." That was his favorite line until Karon bounced back with Ralph's suggestion that if it was such a good business why didn't his wife and mother go into it. The agent, a traditional-thinking Greek, was incensed.

Next door was the branch office of a security firm. There'd been a robbery one day of a truck hauling millions of dollars worth of certificates and bonds. Following a hot tip that it was an inside job, the FBI flooded the office building with agents. They were waiting for the manager of the branch to arrive and stood flush against the hallway, guns drawn, when Karon walked into the hall. "What's going on!" she cried out, then ran back to the office where Joy stood terrified. In a second the men strode in, laughing, explaining the situation.

Out of one of the front offices in the tiny complex, two young men operated a livery service. When business was slow, one would offer to take Karon and Joy to lunch. They often arrived at McDonald's in the back seat of a chauffeur-driven limousine. They loved it, never knew work could be such fun. The local phone man, Bill, came to be a good friend. He was an exuberant, hyperactive man in his early thirties, divorced he said, because he wore his wife out. Sometimes they went to lunch with him too. Joy had finally put her foot down with Gordon. "We have to deal with a lot of different men in this business and whether you like it or not, it has to be that way, so don't give me any trouble." Gordon agreed, but still Joy and Karon were careful. Neither ever went alone with a man, even if for a cup of coffee. "I don't want any gossip," Karon said. "This is all on the up-and-up."

In many instances, the nurses' basic instincts got them by. They agreed, for example, to have Karon's mother and another secretary work part-time answering phones so they could do home visits. But when a woman in the neighborhood volunteered to work free of charge, they declined her offer, concerned about maintaining the confidentiality of their files. It took them a while, however, to think of installing an answering machine to take phone calls and to tape doctors' orders when no one was in the office. They were learning from the basics up, and they were enjoying every minute of it.

They were Registered Professional Nurses, PC. They were in control and they relished the feeling of power and responsibility that went with running their own practice. If they made mistakes, it was in being too conservative and too conscientious. They one time induced a patient's doctor to make a house call for what looked like an obscure scar on the outside of a man's thigh; the affliction turned out to be a simple urine burn. (How'd he get a urine burn *there*? Karon wondered.) And they many times upset their schedules by overstaying on home visits, doing dirty dishes, washing laundry, straightening a patient's room, tasks they weren't paid for but that needed to be done. How many dollars had they spent sending get well cards or calling for flowers when one of their home patients was hospitalized? How many hours had they spent looking at collections of faded photographs, listening to elderly people tell stories of younger, exciting years, stories no one else would listen to?

Their motto was to refuse no one, to take the time for every patient. When a frantic call came in one Sunday morning from a young woman whose mother was having problems, they didn't hesitate to get involved. It seemed serious, said the woman, and the doctor couldn't come out—would they? The nurses arrived at the suburban address to find an immense, sickly woman gurgling in a huge, crankstyle hospital bed that was stationed smack in the middle of the family living room. (Why do people insist on doing that, Karon thought. No wonder the sick are considered such burdens; people make them burdens, putting them center stage.) The daughter was frazzled. "I just don't know what to do anymore," she kept saying. "Mother says it's her stomach so I called the doctor and he prescribed Maalox. That was yesterday and still it's getting worse." Maalox! thought Karon. Sure, Maalox for indigestion, but that's not this woman's problem.

From where the trio stood, near the foot of the patient's bed, Karon and Joy heard the raspy, bubbly breathing, a sound that later, through the stethoscope, would roar like wind in a dense forest. When the nurses examined the stiff, white-haired matriarch they found a highly erratic pulse, swollen ankles from impaired circulation, and an extended, bloated abdomen and

111

chest cavity. "She's practically drowning in her own fluid," Karon whispered to Joy. "She can't stay here like this."

The patient's doctor listened carefully when Karon finally got through to him on the phone. He didn't ask who they thought they were or what business they had attending his patient, he was, it turned out, only concerned about the patient's welfare and grateful for a professional assessment of the situation. "Obviously not indigestion," he remarked. "But those are the symptons the daughter gave me. Why do people think everything is indigestion? I'll call the hospital and have a bed ready for her this afternoon. Thanks."

If only more doctors thought and acted like this one, Karon and Joy said on their way back to the office. If only more of them would think about how we can help them, not see us as threats and mental retards who can't make a step without their direction. We can save them time; we can supplement their own work. This doctor obviously appreciated their input but most, they knew, did not.

Both Karon and Joy felt their experiences in the independent practice were making them better nurses. The new dimension gave them more confidence and a greater understanding of the patients' problems. They were more enthusiastic about nursing than they'd been in years. They were giving more of themselves, not only in their own business but at the hospital as well. They had deliberately set out to insure that their practice would not impose in any way on their jobs at General and they had strived to maintain this attitude. Once the social service department at General asked them to assume the home care of a patient about to be discharged, but this was strictly after hours, an independent business arrangement. It was a point of pride with both women that they never gave the hospital phone number to any of their office patients, that they upheld their good attendance records and continued to receive positive evaluations from their supervisors. More than honor, however, was at stake. Even though Karon and Joy were making the business a financial success, they

112

were drawing no money from it. They needed their hospital salaries as much as they ever had and they knew it.

In their first four months as independent practitioners, Karon and Joy had taken in more money than they'd dreamed possible. They'd aimed for $400 a month and had made nearly four times that much. But their expenses were far greater than their original estimates. Every penny they made was gobbled up by the business. All they'd gotten so far were a few business lunches paid out of petty cash. They knew they'd made mistakes in the money department. Karon who at first had insisted their patients pay in cash only and had wasted valuable time driving around the city to personally pick up payments. Joy who was asked one time to "look in" on a neighbor's mother and did so willingly and then couldn't bring herself to bill the woman for her services.

Although it is difficult to imagine business people hesitant or ineffective in the fee-collecting department, it's important to remember that at heart these two were nurses, *not* business people. Other professionals discuss money up front; Joy and Karon had to force themselves to talk dollars and cents and even when the right words finally tumbled out of their mouths they were cloaked in apologetic tones. When a surburban psychologist repeatedly forgot to pay for the blood tests they'd done on his hypochondriacal wife, it was Karon and Joy who were embarrassed about mentioning the money still owed.

As independent nurse practitioners, they were bucking tradition, prejudice, and a legal system that allowed no room for them. One middle-aged man came to their office for a vitamin B_{12} shot, then balked at their fee. "I'll drive the damn 20 miles to my doctor's office before I'll give you ten dollars for a lousy shot," he said. "Just who the hell do you think you are, anyway?" an angry woman demanded over the phone. "You have no business practicing mail order medicine. What you're doing must be against the law."

A young woman who went to a local internist weekly for two shots wanted to switch to Registered Professional Nurses because the nurses' office was more convenient for her. The doctor said she could, but would give her a prescription for only one of the shots needed. When Joy called the doctor to ask for the other order, he refused to give it to her. "I want my patient to come here," he said. The girl had no choice. The doctor wanted her weekly $15 and didn't care about the time she spent waiting every Tuesday morning in his office; he didn't care that for less money and no waiting time she could have the same procedure done at Registered Professional Nurses as his nurse did in his office. "Does he do anything else for you?" Karon asked the young woman. "His nurse takes my blood pressure and he always asks how I'm feeling. That's all."

Another time Karon and Joy were dropped from a case because the family couldn't afford to pay them without some reimbursement from the government. Even though the woman's doctor, a psychiatrist, recommended the treatment, and Karon and Joy were, as far as they knew, the only nursing service in the state to provide at-home psychiatric care, Medicare would not approve payment for their visits.

Karon and Joy were not charging enough for their services, but they didn't realize this yet. The only solution they saw to their money situation was to promote even more business, to expand in new and different ways so they could do more work themselves and also contract with other nurses, paying them a set amount and keeping the rest as their fee. They were determined to leave nothing untried. They believed that just because something hadn't been done in the past didn't mean it wouldn't work for them.

Karon sent out a series of letters to area saving and loan associations suggesting they hire Registered Professional Nurses to provide a mini-health-screening service for customers: $2 for blood pressure readings and $1 for a diabetes test. "You may be interested in using this as one of your savings promotions offered to new savers as the first of its kind," she wrote. "Save Money, Save Your Health, Stay Alive and Save More" was the motto she

114

suggested. None of the financial institutions were interested. She contacted local cemeteries and tried to sell them the idea of pre-employment physical exams for their staff. Nothing came from this, either. She approached the labyrinthine Chicago Board of Education, offering to do onsite screening of teachers, and got a polite refusal for her efforts. Karon even went after the Chicago Police Department, but to no avail.

Joy and Karon were fighting the system and its ingrown ways of doing business; they were outsiders looking in, too new perhaps to be taken seriously. Woman as business owners were not yet a hot item in 1974. Independent nurse practitioners were still virtually unheard of. "Every nurse is, in reality, an independent practitioner," Karon and Joy would carefully explain to the skeptics, who continued to walk away with raised eyebrows and smirks on their faces.

Every once in a while, though, something new came their way. They were able to negotiate a strong contract with the head office of an insurance agency allowing them to perform all the insurance physicals for the company in the Chicago area. They submitted a bid to provide onsite first aid and medical care for the construction crew building a warehouse for the National Tea Company. After five weeks of negotiating, the insurance carrier and the builder agreed to a two-year verbal contract giving Registered Professional Nurses the job. Karon and Joy immediately turned around and subcontracted the job to two nurse friends who were looking for work. Each month Marge and Stella billed Registered Professional Nurses for their services and every month Karon and Joy billed the construction company. "This could lead to big stuff," Karon told Joy one day after she heard from someone that every large building site more than four miles from a hospital was required by the Occupational Safety and Health Act to have a nurse on the premises. "Think of all the construction that goes on around here. I want you to start writing down names of any businesses you see being built. We'll contact them all." And they did, but no more construction jobs came.

115

Initially, Karon had done the promotional work involved with the business, mainly because she enjoyed doing it and Joy did not. But one person devoting only a few hours a day to publicity efforts wasn't enough. Like it or not, Joy had to get involved. She started by convincing the manager of a local drug store to let them conduct a one-day blood pressure and diabetes health screening program on his premises. "He says okay but only if we sit in the display window," Joy said when she got off the phone. And that's just what the two nurses did for half a day as patrons came and went.

Joy also contracted with the women's auxiliary of one of the suburban fire departments to give blood tests and blood pressure measurements to the entire force. Financially, the arrangement was tilted in favor of the department, but the nurses felt the publicity was worth the difference. So for $10 per person (the lab work cost $7 per patient), they piled equipment in their car, scraped an inch-thick coat of ice off the windshield, shoveled out the back wheels, and drove through a near blizzard to draw blood for typing and to wrap the biceps of fifty men, every one of whom had ridiculously high blood pressure levels because he'd been out shoveling snow. At no extra charge, the nurses had to repeat their work.

Karon and Joy were learning about the power of the press and they worked for every bit of media coverage and attention they could get. The *Congressional Record* included nearly a full page on their innovative service. The *Chicago Sun Times*, *The Suburban Week News*, and two other area papers ran stories. So did the *American Journal of Nursing*. In *McCalls* and the *Reader's Digest* they were delighted with short clips—reminiscent of the one-paragraph story that had helped spur them on.

The nurse practitioners would do anything to promote the business. They gave free blood pressure tests to a local senior citizens' group as a way of introducing themselves to the organization. They sat in the middle of a K-Mart discount store while the manager's voice broke through the grating Musak to announce

116

that, as a special service to customers, two registered nurses were waiting to take their blood pressure measurements. "It's a blue light special," he kept saying, and all the while he talked a crazy blue light, looking like it was stolen from a police car and then dangled by a single wire from the overhead framework, flashed over their heads.

Karon and Joy knew that hard work would, in large part, determine the success of their business and their future as independent nurses. But work wasn't a guarantee. There were other factors they could not control. One was a free clinic that had opened down the street shortly after Registered Professional Nurses went into operation. The clinic was funded under a state and federal revenue-sharing program. It had a doctor on the premises but in many respects its scope was limited compared to Karon and Joy's. "We'll work together," Karon insisted, her faith running high, and off she went to negotiate, asking for home visits on a referral basis and volunteering to recommend some of their patients to the clinic's physician. It was an amicable arrangement, but, they would learn later, only a temporary one.

Another, more serious, threat loomed, one the nurses had failed to see. It was a threat that could undermine their entire professional standing, jeopardizing both their nursing careers and their independent practice.

chapter eight

On October 9, 1974, thirteen months after Joy and Karon opened their independent nursing practice, the bottom virtually dropped out. The Director of Nursing at General Community Hospital called Karon at home late that morning and told her she was to report with Joy to her office in the afternoon. When the nurses showed up, they were told they'd been fired, abruptly and summarily dismissed from their nursing positions at General. Karon had been employed at the hospital for five and a half years, Joy for seven. During that time, they had consistently received excellent evaluations from their superiors. Their records were free from any official reprimand; never had either been censured for any action. In fact, just two weeks prior to this startling development, Joy had earned top marks from the departmental supervisor. And Karon had recently been asked to consider a supervisory role in the new wing of the hospital.

Now both stood accused of being uncooperative and of disrupting service and morale in the psych ward. They were labeled instigators, nurses who put their own interests above those of the patients and the hospital. The dismissal did not take place calmly. Voices were raised and angry words exchanged. When Joy and Karon left the office of the Director of Nursing, their heads were spinning. Either none of it made sense or it all added up too perfectly, creating a picture the two women could not believe or accept. It would take them months to sort out the pieces and to understand their true feelings toward the event and the people involved. Until then, they were quite literally wounded, their psyches and emotions torn by shame and humiliation.

Earned or not, the burden of guilt was dropped unceremoniously at their feet. They were convinced that no matter what they said, people would not believe them.

Lurking behind the sympathetic nods and the comforting words were the unspoken accusations and suspicions. Everyone would assume they had been fired because they were incompetent, because they were not good nurses. Tradition, the structure of society, maybe even human nature were all working against them. Karon and Joy knew it, and because of this and because they believed so strongly in their innocence and in the record of their professional accomplishments, they became obsessed. They would not accept what had happened. They would not rest until they were vindicated.

* * * * *

Maybe they should have seen it coming. For months they wondered how they'd been so blind or their vision so crowded with other images that the ax had come with such surprise. True, Karon had been busier than ever before in her life. In addition to becoming a businesswoman in the previous year, she'd also become a mother. The timing couldn't have been worse. The day after she and Joy opened the doors of Registered Professional Nurses, Ralph had received a phone call from his daughter, Becky. "Can you come get me?" she asked. "I want to live with you and Karon." And of course Ralph went. Suddenly there were rock records on the stereo, a second hair dryer in the bathroom, and jeans everywhere in the apartment. Surprisingly, Karon didn't mind. She liked Becky, liked especially the fact that if she was going to have a child around it was not one in diapers but one who could talk and reason and accept some responsibility for her own care.

Karon set rules for study and entertaining, encouraged her brothers to become friends with the girl, and found she enjoyed the shopping forays and movies and dinners out that now included Ralph's daughter. Becky was a good kid and Karon, who had never

119

been partial to the child's mother, felt a responsibility toward the young teenager. "She hasn't had an easy life," Karon said to Joy once. "And I guess we owe it to her to help out the best we can." Sometimes Becky even babysat for Joy or was invited along when Joy took her own daughters out.

As far as Karon was concerned, the main difference Becky had made in her life was that she finally stepped down from her full-time slot at the hospital to a four-day work week. It happened in April, 1974, when Karon's doctor insisted she ease up temporarily on her schedule and wrote a letter to that effect, which Karon passed on to her superiors. With it, Karon relinquished her role as charge nurse on the second shift. She wasn't entirely displeased but considered it only a short-term arrangement and would not realize until later the impact this move would have on her eventual dismissal.

The same month Karon went to four days. Joy faced her own personal turning point. She had an argument with Gordon, the worst ever, and she decided finally to leave him. She was going to call the lawyer in the morning, had her mind set, but then she told her husband and the disagreement that had been the worst ever was surpassed by the subsequent argument. By midnight Gordon was sitting at the station house (Joy had called the police—her husband's friends—and asked them just to get him out of the house for a while), and Joy was near hysterics. If she ever hated Gordon it was probably that night, but ironically, there she was, sifting through papers and documents looking for his gun registration, wondering why she could not sit back and let him get in trouble. It wasn't her fault the police thought his gun was stolen. (They'd asked to see the weapon as a matter of course when they arrived. This is ridiculous, Joy thought; he wears the damn thing every day.) She eventually found the papers, phoned the station, and got Gordon off the hook.

When Joy was able to begin rethinking the confusion in her mind, the phone began ringing. Every half hour Gordon called. He loved her. He loved the children. He wouldn't drink anymore. Wouldn't she stay? Wouldn't she give him another chance? By morning, when she drove to the station to pick him up, Joy had decided. For the sake of the children she would stay. Until the youngest was grown she would remain in this house, with this man. Then she would leave, would have no qualms about leaving. In her heart, though, she was gone already; she was free. It was a small gesture, perhaps but it was all Joy could do, to remove her gold wedding band, to vow never to put it on again. She would never cheat on Gordon, she knew, but somehow having the ring off lifted a weight. Joy felt expansive that morning, ready to get on with the business of living. Sure, she'd do the laundry and fix the meals and clean the house—everything just as she'd always done—but now she had what she'd never had before, a light at the end of the tunnel, and she'd hurry toward it eagerly.

These events made Karon and Joy perhaps a little more complacent about their jobs at the hospital, the big white womb they hurried to and hurried out of like clockwork, as always. Over a series of months, different problems had been cropping up. While these might not have contributed directly to the firing, they did add to the growing atmosphere of discontent that had been brewing among the staff at General.

The hospital had recently begun a new building program, not a conservative project but a massive undertaking that would nearly double the capacity of the facility. While building-fund drives were going on throughout the community, and among the employees, economy moves were instituted internally and staff numbers were either cut or allowed to dwindle through attrition. Simultaneously, the first rumblings of women and nurse employment complaints were being heard. As mere whispers of dissent and barely audible requests for more personnel, better working conditions, and more self-direction were surfacing, the hospital administrators were marshalling funds in the direction of bricks and mortar; they were too busy, perhaps, to listen to complaints. For whatever reasons tempers were short and defenses were up; the working climate had changed.

One of the first clues had come that previous winter when a rehab nurse called in sick, leaving a ward unattended. "You take charge," the supervisor told Karon. Logistically, it was an obvious move—Karon and psych were on 7E, rehab was on 7W. Legally, and from a common sense point of view, it was a poor choice.

"I'm in charge of a locked unit and if I leave there's no RN here, only an aide. I won't do that," Karon said.

"You do it, or I'll have your job."

"No, I can't do it. It's illegal. I will be available to any patient who needs me, but I will not be responsible for patients outside a locked ward." Do it yourself, Karon thought, you aren't doing anything else. Aloud she added, "If you insist on my doing it, I'll report you—then we'll see whose job it is." (Later the supervisor did complain about Karon's actions but was told by the nursing office that Karon had been correct to refuse to leave her ward under the circumstances.)

Not long after, in January, 1974, Karon's father suffered a heart attack. He was rushed to the emergency room at General, directly from his doctor's office, where his EKG registered abnormal activity. But instead of being assigned a bed in the ER or being sent directly to a room for observation, Mr. White was directed to the admitting office (apparently to clarify some confusion over his records). At the time General was already expanding. The new construction meant old hallways were blocked off and passageways were rerouted. No one in ER called the admission office for Karon's father, nor did anyone offer him a wheelchair ride. No, he was told to walk, even though his doctor had called in specific orders prior to his arrival. He had to follow the yellow line, to be exact (the line was used to guide people through the construction maze) upstairs, downstairs, around and about corridors until a city block later he was at the admit office. Karon learned of the incident later in the day and was furious. "He could have been having a heart attack parading through that damn hospital," she screamed to Ralph. "I'm going to find out about this!" So she called the emergency room and asked who was responsible.

"I don't know who it was," the voice said.

"Can you find out for me, please?"

"Listen here, madam," the voice said, "that's none of your business."

Karon—by now on the edge of her chair—asked whom she was speaking to.

"Madam, I am not giving you my name."

"Don't 'madam' me and don't get smart either. I happen to be a nurse at General and *never* in five years have I been ashamed to give my name to anyone."

At which point Karon gave her name and asked again whom she was talking with.

"I don't have to tell you anything," the voice said, and put the phone on hold.

After talking to another nurse who also refused to identify herself, Karon finally reached the person in charge and related the entire incident. In addition to complaining about the reception her father had been given, she made the point that if ER nurses treated the public the way they treated her, then the hospital's image was going to be in real trouble. "I'll check into it," the charge nurse said, and Karon, busy with her practice, and worried about her father, dismissed it—though she would remember the incident months later when words like "troublemaker" rang through the director's office.

There were, at General, some nurses who wanted change and some who wanted a union (not always the same people). Someone suggested that the best way to build the groundwork for future organizing activity was first to get a large group of nurses rallied around a cause and then confront the hospital with the situation. According to the scenario, the hospital administrators would recognize the validity of the cause and the nurses' right to negotiate on behalf of their own welfare. Once the nurses realized the power of standing together, once they got a feel for their collective might, they would transform naturally into union-thinking people.

123

Thus the petition that evolved said nothing about unions. Rather, it detailed a number of fairly routine requests and pointed out areas of common concern. Among other things, the petition asked for the establishment of a grievance committee; for additional staff, every third weekend off, improved health benefits (full-time nurses at General received one sick day for every month worked; part-time nurses had prorated sick days but no hospitalization insurance); an investigation into what was described as "tremendous employee turnover"; and alleviation of the parking situation (putting more lights in the lots and allowing the second- and third-shift nurses to park closer to the hospital for safety reasons). The petition was not very sophisticated, but it represented a start.

Joy and Karon knew about the petition and the rumblings behind it, but they stayed clear, guilty of a certain amount of apathy (they were busy with their new business and they were basically happy with the arrangements on their unit now), and, in Karon's case, a little suspicious. When the organizers asked her to take charge of getting signatures for the petition, Karon said no. "I already have a reputation for speaking out and they probably think I'm too independent now with the business, so really I'd be more likely to hurt your cause than to help it. They might think I was planning to leave and just wanting to start trouble first." But she told the organizers that if they were really serious and were willing to each donate $50 "for the lawyer I'll need after presenting that thing to the administration," then she would do it. The nurses balked and Karon turned away.

Christine did not. Christine was a venoclysis or IV therapy nurse, one who traveled from floor to floor throughout her work day. Because of her mobility, she was the perfect carrier for the petition. The petition itself didn't mean that much to Christine, although she agreed with its points; she thought the protest all rather innocent. Of course she would help out; why not? was her attitude. Later, when Karon and Joy learned that Christine was circulating the petition, they tried to warn her. Christine had done some work for them through Registered Professional Nurses and they didn't want to see her hurt. "Nurses always back off. They jack you up to do it and then they back off," Karon told her. But Christine wouldn't listen.

So the petition went out, with a blank sheet of paper attached, because, in the end, the old fears were the strongest. The nurses at General were so afraid to sign the actual grievance document that, instead, they signed the blank sheet. (So, if trouble developed, later they could argue that they hadn't known what they were signing.) This wasn't the only precaution taken. Those who signed did not write their names in the prescribed fashion. No one wanted to be first on the list. Signatures were scrawled sideways, upside down, in a circle, until the paper looked like a kindergarten art project. How anyone expected such a weak show of force to win out is almost laughable in retrospect, but they did. And they were fooled.

The administration heard about the activities, of course, and told Christine to stop circulating the petition (in fact, they accused her of using force to coerce people into signing). Christine refused, and she was fired. Effective immediately. Bounced out the door. Christine with two teenaged children, the still mortgaged house in the suburbs, the ex-husband who forgot his support payments more often than he remembered them. Christine was sent packing. So effective was the message from on high that not a single nurse in the entire hospital went to Christine's defense. Not one stood up and said, "I signed the petition; fire me too." Not one voice cried, "Unfair!" or reminded the director that Christine had been a fine nurse who did her work well.

Silence and fear took over. There was one meeting with the Illinois Nurses Association to discuss the situation. Karon and Joy went to it; they had to because Christine was a friend and she'd been hurt. When that happens, they knew, you don't sit back and do nothing. But little came of the gathering and any hope of a meaningful follow-up fizzled.

Meanwhile, the hospital management responded in its own

way to the petition and the grievances it expressed. One evening during the change of shifts, a group of administrators hid in the laundry room and conducted their own survey of the nurses' parking lot, presumably to check safety and see if, in fact, the area was poorly lighted. Then the hospital set up a series of meetings to listen to "legitimate" complaints. It was one of those "we'll show the peons we really do care" moves and it worked. Until someone spotted the secretary in the back of the room taking down the name of any nurse who actually did speak out. Soon there were no complaints and no more meetings. Just a few hundred women with their heads in the sand, doing their jobs.

* * * * *

Immediately after leaving the director's office, stripped of title, job, seniority, all they'd worked for over the years, Karon and Joy got into a car and drove 150 miles to a gathering of the Illinois League of Nursing. They were scheduled speakers, had been invited months before to talk about the problems of running an independent practice. Neither had yet prepared a speech, but at this point, who cared? Joy, the driver, was crying. Karon, the passenger, was thinking out loud.

"It had to be that bitch Louise. She was finally going to get even with me for all those years I reported her activities. So she goes to Mrs. T. whining, 'Those girls! How can I make up a schedule when they keep requesting days off?' I can just hear her now. Make a pauper a prince and it goes right to the old head."

About the time Karon had reduced her schedule to four days, Louise Rowland, someone she had been warned about nearly four years earlier, was made a temporary charge nurse on the day shift. Finally Louise had more power than Karon, but it wasn't until October that their paths crossed. With the head nurse and the supervisor both off, Louise had control of scheduling. It was then the agreement between Karon and Joy and the other two nurses working the second shift on psych came to her attention.

On their own the independent practitioners had offered to work

126

four weekends in a row and to take their free days during the Monday to Friday portion of the week. They needed this schedule for their business and for two speaking engagements. (They were about to appear before the National Joint Practice Commission, as well as at the Illinois League for Nursing. "Shouldn't a hospital be *proud* its nurses are asked to speak to professional groups? Don't you think they'd encourage this?" Karon asked Joy on their drive.) They knew most staff nurses covet free weekends, that one of the long-standing complaints was having to work on Saturdays and Sundays on a regular basis. ("We're doing people a favor and we get kicked in the teeth.")

They were out of the city now, rolling through the Illinois harvest country, heading south.

Anyway, the other two nurses had agreed: Joy and Karon would work weekends for four consecutive weeks, then would get the next two weekends off. The other two nurses would have four consecutive free weekends, then would work the following two. Karon wrote a note to that effect and passed it along to the supervisor.

This morning she and Joy had seen the note again. It was waving in the hands of the Director of Nursing, who had called them both in that day specifically to discuss the situation.

Again, Karon and Joy played the scene back as they remembered it.

Accused of causing scheduling problems, they had explained their arrangement. They could see the director was hot, her nurses, her darling nurses of all those years suddenly going haywire. For years no problems, no unions, petitions, going off on their own; where would it all lead? What happened to the good old days of harmony and peace, when nurses were nice quiet ladies who never talked back?

"They agreed?" the director asked.

The Director of Personnel was there. The door was open and the voices were loud enough for the secretaries outside to hear.

"Yes," Karon said.

"Okay, we'll get them down from the floor and see." The director buzzed her secretary and told her to find the other two nurses. Then she turned to Karon and Joy. "You will be fired depending on what they say. If they say they didn't agree to this, you will be fired."

A tense silence followed, but neither Karon nor Joy was worried. They were confused and angered by what was happening but not worried. They'd been so careful all along. They had gone out of their way, as far as they could tell, not to let their business interfere with their work here, had been conscientious almost to the point of being fanatical. No, they had nothing to worry about. Certainly, there was no hard feelings between them and the other two nurses. Hadn't the four of them gone together to the meeting about Christine's firing? One of the women had even offered to fix Joy's hair for her at home, when Joy had the time to play around with a new style. Nothing to worry about, except maybe getting a late start on their trip to Peoria. Karon glanced at her watch. They were an hour behind schedule already.

Suddenly it was over. The other nurses had arrived. The director had asked point blank: "Did you see this paper—yes or no? Did you ever see this paper?" And they had answered. No. And Karon had sprung up, a knot tightening in her stomach and reaching up threatening to strangle her. Why hadn't she thought of that? Of course they had not seen the paper. *She* had written the note. But they had agreed to the contents, at least to the portion about the weekend arrangement; the other requests in the note didn't concern them. Karon tried to argue the point but the director waved away her objections, had acted as if she didn't hear the nurses say, Yes, they'd agreed to taking those particular weekends off. "Did you see this paper?" she asked them again. "No," they answered again, and were dismissed.

The actual firing came in a hailstorm of accusations and arguments. At one point Karon and Joy heard the director call them liars and troublemakers. "If my standing up for things makes me a troublemaker, then I'm proud of it," Karon bellowed. "But *her*,"

pointing to Joy, "she never did anything. Why are you firing her?"
The director said something about being on the wrong team.
"What team? I didn't know anything about teams," Joy replied.
Then Mrs. T. said she had affidavits from other nurses stating they
refused to work with Karon and Joy. "Where are they? Let's see
them," Joy demanded, but the director ignored her.

In less than twenty minutes, it was all over. The head of
personnel had heard every word and probably half the nursing
staff knew about it before long.

"We'll see you in court," Karon said on her way through the
door.

"You're all her puppets. You're her puppets," Joy sang out to
the group of nursing supervisors and secretaries who sat outside
the director's office, staring at the two in shock.

"She called me a liar. Two months ago after the meeting over
Christine, she stopped me in the hall and said, 'Gibson, did you
have anything to do with this petition?' And when I said no, she
said she knew I was telling the truth because she knew I'd never
lie to her. Then hugged me! Now she calls me a liar in front of a half
dozen people."

Karon and Joy had finally reached Peoria and were bombarding
two nurses who had the adjoining hotel room with their story. Joy
still could barely bring herself to talk about the events of the
afternoon. Karon could do nothing else. "You know what I heard?
People said she was jealous and maybe scared. She figured everything is going great guns with our business, that we have the
ability to get on TV and in newspapers, and that we're just getting
too powerful and it's only a matter of time before we do start
getting into this union business." Karon lit a cigarette and paced
across the room. "You know, I was probably one of the most
conservative nurses in that place. Can you believe that? I followed
the rules religiously. I believed in the rules. I was the one who
reported the nurses for drinking on the floor during the Christmas
party last year. Boy, were they mad over that! 'It's Christmas,'
they said, 'It's special.' I didn't care. People still have heart attacks

on Christmas, and who wants a drunk nurse bending over trying to save his life? And I'm the one who gets fired—not the ones who were drinking."

The other nurses nodded politely; they wanted to hear more. "Do you know what people will think—they'll think we killed somebody! That's what people think when nurses get fired, that they maimed someone or killed a patient. My God, our reputations will go right down the drain."

"She said I used the hospital phone to make calls for business," Joy broke in, her voice thin and high-pitched. "I never did that. She said she had complaints that I made unfair requests of the scheduler. Karon was the scheduler."

"Our outside interest interfered with our work, that's what she said," Karon began talking again. "Every doctor in that hospital has a practice—isn't that an outside interest? We know about doctors who go for a week without showing up to see their patients! I worked with an orderly once who had permission to sleep during our shift because he had another job during the day. There's a male nurse there who has another full-time nursing job. Outside interest, nuts. They just didn't like that we were finally doing something, we were showing nurses they don't need that umbilical cord to the hospital."

Midnight came and the other two nurses went to bed. Karon and Joy were alone, trying to talk their way out of their misery. Their anxiety worked on their bodies, their minds, their spirits. The world that only yesterday was filled with purpose and direction was now dismal. Sure they would have more time for their business now—hadn't Joy been trying to convince Karon only a couple of weeks earlier they should quit and do the independent practice full time?—but that wasn't the point. They had been wronged, their reputation had been harmed. Plus the reality was that they still needed the money from other employment. The business was taking care of itself financially, but it wasn't paying them salaries yet. How could the two of them apply now for jobs at other hospitals? They felt they couldn't, not with ease or confi-

130

dence, not with this awful black cloud hanging over their starched white caps. What kind of references would they get from General? They could only guess.

For months both Karon and Joy would have nightmares, would wake at strange hours of the morning feeling despair and guilt. Guilt because they had failed, which was the way the world would perceive the situation. Karon's grandmother demonstrated this painfully well. She had listened carefully when Karon first broke the news to the family; she had been sympathetic and considerate. Yet months later she would turn to her granddaughter and say, "Now Karon, tell me what really happened." If her own grandmother felt that way, Karon thought, what hope was there for them?

The next morning in Peoria, Karon and Joy took turns standing before an audience of nurses and medical professionals eager to hear about the work involved in establishing an independent practice. This was a proud moment for the two women. Their hearts should have been dancing, not weeping. Their faces triumphant, not tortured. "Until recently, nursing has been a rather restricted profession," Karon began. "It was neatly packaged into the areas of hospitals, physicians' offices, schools, and private-duty nursing. These limitations, which we seem to have willingly placed on ourselves, have tended to rob the profession and society of the full benefits and rewards nursing as a profession has to offer. I refer specifically to the independent practice of nursing. . . ."

There are a lot of important people in this room, Karon thought, even as she was speaking. They should know about what happened to us, because of the practice. Someone is bound to get incensed and do something about it, someone who has more connections than we do. So at the end of her talk, Karon related the events of the previous day, watching the headshaking and whispering. But that was it, the extent of the response. No offers to help, no advice or consolation, no indignities expressed, no sense of camaraderie. Karon and Joy had gone out on the limb alone, and when the branch cracked they were left to fall alone.

"What are we going to do?" Joy asked on the drive home, wishing she were headed farther away from, not back toward, their troubles.

"I don't know, Joy," Karon said. "But something, that's for sure. We'll think of something."

chapter nine

*I*n their battle to clear their professional names, Karon and Joy felt weak, like lilliputians in a land of giants, two lone nurses, in disgrace, fighting the good guy in town.

Except they had faith. They sincerely believed they were in the right, that their professional reputations had been smeared and that they had been callously and unjustly treated. Perhaps if they'd never had any experience outside their nursing jobs at the hospital, they would have given in, simply shrugged their shoulders, bowed their heads in embarrassment, and walked away. But if nothing else, their independent practice had taught Joy and Karon that an individual with a dream and the sheer guts and will power to work for that dream has a chance.

Besides, they had each other. Alone, this would be a long, miserable struggle; together, it would be as arduous but there would be more strength on their side. For Joy and Karon, one plus one added up to the force of ten.

While the nurses knew what they wanted to accomplish—to clear their names and to force the hospital into acknowledging its error—they had no idea how to do it. One week after being fired, they had tried talking to the chief administrator at General. He met them with another unidentified party present, and said he couldn't believe the things they were telling him. "I'll look into it and get back to you," he promised. But Karon and Joy never heard from him again. So they tried writing to the hospital's Chairman of the Board. His response was that he couldn't get involved with the day-to-day activities of the institution. Finally, on their third try, they went to their lawyer, who wrote the hospital requesting that

133

Joy and Karon be reinstated or legal action would follow. There was no response, and the lawyer, whose expertise ran more to corporate law, begged off from further involvement. This was just as well, since Karon and Joy had begun to realize that for $3,000 in legal fees they gotten very little in return. (One bill listed $250 worth of phone calls supposedly made by Joy on days and at times she couldn't possibly have called. "You want to earn $250 on phone calls," she told the lawyer. "I'll call you and make you talk to me for five hours. Then you can send me a bill like this.") They learned the name of the attorney for the Illinois Nurses Association and went to see him.

For two days they conferred with the INA attorney. Karon and Joy wanted to go to the Equal Employment Opportunity Commission with a sex discrimination complaint. The lawyer said no, they wouldn't have a prayer; try the National Labor Relations Board and tie in the alleged union activities. He helped draft a letter requesting a review and an appeal of their discharge from General Community Hospital. That was in November, 1974.

"This'll do it, you'll see," Karon told Joy, as they settled in for what they'd been told would be a long wait.

In December they received word from the NLRB that there was insufficient reason to link the firing to union activities. The lawyer said he could do no more and Karon and Joy were once again adrift.

As they had done so many times before, the two women went into action on their own, willing to make mistakes and learn from them, but determined to see the issue through. "We aren't smoke blowers, just remember that," Karon kept saying. Despite the attorney's advice on the sex discrimination argument, Karon and Joy were sure they could win on it. They based their reasoning on the fact that General had hired a male, licensed practical nurse a few years before who worked full-time while attending school for his RN diploma. The man, who had nine children, quit for a short period, then returned as a registered nurse four days a week while holding down a full-time job at a local mental health center and studying for a bachelor's degree at a nearby college. They had been told, by people who worked the night shift with him, that he had permission to sleep while on duty, had been issued written notices about absenteeism, and had a number of less-than-perfect evaluations on file. Yet he was still employed at General when they had been fired. "Enough is enough," the two women agreed, and in late December, squeaking in under the 90-day deadline, they filed a complaint with the EEOC.

On Christmas Eve, the local NBC news team filmed Karon and Joy doing an insurance physical and for a few hours their spirits rose. The media interest gave them a shot of hope and reinforced in their own eyes the importance of what they were doing as independent practitioners. TV exposure would do more for them than a two-hour stint taking blood pressures at the neighborhood Walgreen's drug store, which was their next stop that day. "What a way to spend Christmas Eve," Joy said, as she and Karon set up their card table stand amid the red and green glitter draped throughout the store. Walgreen's did a good business that night, what with the hordes of last-minute shoppers grabbing for gift boxes of perfume, after-shave lotion, and candy. Registered Professional Nurses didn't do as well. Blood pressures were not a big item that night of the year, and Karon and Joy had to settle for handing out their business cards and wishing people a Merry Christmas.

January went by and the heavy gloom so typical of Midwestern winters wafted over Karon and Joy. At first they were sure the EEOC would save them, that someone at the agency would quickly set all wrongs straight. But soon they learned government wheels don't move that way. Weeks dragged by, snow piled up, and finally a letter arrived aknowledging receipt of their complaint. Karon learned, in talking to the investigator assigned to their case, that the procedure could take years to complete. This was like a death knell to Karon and Joy, and so again they reached out on their own. They were convinced that the Director of Nursing who'd fired them acted unethically by impugning their integrity in front of other hospital personnel. Karon wrote to the Illinois Division of Nursing, Department of Registration and Education, about the matter. "The purpose of this letter is to register a complaint we would appreciate your department investigating against a Registered Nurse; yet we would like to do it without unjustly defaming the Nurse we have the complaint about. . . ."

The correspondence was dated February 6; on February 14, they had their reply. "Your letter was evaluated in relation to the Illinois Nursing Act, Section 15 and in my judgment does not fall within our domain."

Joy and Karon were growing immune to such rejections and reversals. Long before, their business had taught them not to take such obstacles personally. The people writing these letters and making all the seemingly harsh, negative decisions in the world were doing a job, filling a function, staying safely within the limits some other bureaucrat had drawn. It had nothing to do with Karon and Joy as individuals and, they felt, reflected no less on the validity of their cause than a rejection from a construction firm did on the level of their nursing ability. Too many people were broken down by the system; they would not be.

Thus, eleven days after the disappointing letter from the Department of Registration and Education arrived, Karon and Joy again took up the gauntlet with the NLRB, requesting a review and an appeal of their case. On March 9, they even wrote to the Secretary of Labor, in care of the federal building in downtown Chicago, only to be told, "This particular office is unable to assist you." In April the NLRB again said no. (A local newspaper carried a story about the decision and one patient in the office that day quipped "That's the strangest kind of advertising I've seen yet.") Suddenly, the nurses found themselves with their eggs in one basket, that of the EEOC.

At some point during the winter, Karon and Joy realized there was another resource available to them. One they knew nothing about, had never used, and in fact had often looked down upon. Should they go for help was a question they agonized over for

136

weeks. Finally, the two women, who had never been what they called "women libbers," swallowed their pride and began calling local women's groups. They knew they needed guidance, and while some assistance was coming from the established segments of society, it was qualified help, tainted with condescension and gloom. They wanted *enthusiasm* and began to feel the first stirrings of the common cause that was drawing women everywhere together.

One day Karon and Joy called the Chicago office of NOW, the National Organization of Women, and were told about a Thursday evening, phone-in legal workshop that might prove helpful. When Thursday came around, Karon called again and talked to a representative from a local group entitled DARE (Direct Action for Rights in Employment), a small organization that at the time was working to help city hall matrons in a bid for equal pay and job status with men holding similar jobs. The DARE women were lawyers, paralegals, teachers, secretaries, a small cohesive core, well-organized and deeply dedicated to one cause: other women. That evening the spokesperson listened to Karon and Joy's story. Shortly afterward, the nurses received a call inviting them to a DARE meeting to discuss the situation further.

Like models of Middle America, hair set, makeup in place, outfits coordinated, Karon and Joy walked into a third-floor crash pad. Everyone else in the room wore flannel shirts and jeans—not the Gloria Vanderbilt and Sasson styles of the late Seventies, but the worn and patched, faded pants of the people's armies of protest. There were only two chairs in the living room and Karon and Joy perched on them uncomfortably while the 15 other women sat easily on the large pillows strewn about the floor. Joy spotted a plain, hard mattress set on the floor of another room; she had never seen anything like that before and found her eye constantly wandering back to it. Both she and Karon half expected an explanation—someone was just moving in or out, the decorators were coming in the morning, anything would have been welcome. But the DARE women said nothing, and in minutes it was obvious that this milieu, so foreign to the two nurses, was commonplace to them.

Karon and Joy realized, self-consciously, that these were the very type of people they would have called weirdos had they met them on the street. But the nurses, who were the seekers, had no choice but to hold their tongues and stay put.

Karon did most of the talking that evening, relating, and as she did, reliving, the events of the previous October that had ended in their dismissal from General. For the first time the nurses met with an enthusiastic response to their plight. DARE members were outraged; they asked questions, took notes, immediately offered to write a protest pamphlet and to hand out leaflets at the hospital.

"What if you get arrested?" Karon asked.

"We're prepared to be arrested," they answered.

And when Karon and Joy both admitted they were terrified of that possibility they were told not to worry. "You two don't even have to be part of it. We'll take care of it."

When the nurses walked out the front door of the old brick building late that night, they were in a daze. For so long, it seemed, they'd had to create the whirlwind of activity and noisy protest around their dismissal. The others they'd gone to—all men—had been courteous but distant, seeming to prefer that the entire matter be swept under a convenient hearth rug. Now to have this happen, to have someone else voluntarily lift the burden, even if only temporarily, was almost intoxicating.

In their hearts, Karon and Joy had felt scorn for the old surroundings and sloppy clothes of the women in the tiny, unfurnished apartment. A week later the independent practitioners were humbled. On two of the coldest, windiest days of winter—with temperatures well below zero and a brutal wind blowing—the DARE women, five in each group, leafleted General Community Hospital, distributing pink protest sheets that proclaimed, "Power goes to two poles. One to the people. One to the people with money!" The picketers knew their business. They were careful to stand on the public sidewalk and not put a foot on hospital property. When a hospital administrator came out and threatened to call the police, they urged him to do so, knowing that with the police would come the reporters. The man went back inside and did nothing.

Not far away, Karon and Joy sat in the warm comfort of Karon's car. Both of them felt guilty about not giving out leaflets too, but their fear of arrest was greater than their guilt. They could not believe that these women—all strangers to them except for their one meeting the week before—had come from throughout the city to help, had arranged for babysitters and ridden buses and trains in the worst commuting season, to stand by other women in need.

"Our best friends wouldn't have done that," Karon remarked later and Joy agreed. In fact, even as the two sat on the outskirts of the scene, nurses they knew from the hospital walked past and wouldn't look in their direction. Although this angered Karon and Joy, they understood. Weren't they still a little afraid too? Why hadn't they admitted some allegiance when the local police cruiser had pulled up and the officer asked, "You with them?" He'd laughed, then, at their negative answer and pointed to the leaflets stacked on the dashboard, and they had laughed too, but awkwardly.

None of this, however, seemed to bother the DARE women. They were, no doubt, accustomed to derision and fear and hesitancy. They had no time for any of that. Occasionally, one would pop into Karon's car to warm up, but mostly they marched and worked as promised.

For all their efforts, the DARE protestors would not accept any donations of money from Karon and Joy. They had volunteered for the job, they said; they asked nothing in return. This was their cause as much as anyone else's. All Karon and Joy could do was take the morning shift out to breakfast, then bid them all farewell.

Basically, the DARE alliance ended there. Karon called one of the women every now and then to let her know of progress in their appeals and the complaints being filed, but one day she got a recording saying the number had been disconnected. and she never heard from or about the group again. Who knows if the protest accomplished anything on a large scale that winter? Probably it did not, although it certainly helped make visible women in action working for other women, if anyone bothered to look. There was impact in one quarter, however. If DARE did nothing else those two days, it converted Karon White Gibson and Joy Smith Catterson to the cause of women's liberation. For the first time Joy and Karon really understood what women's lib was all about. A sense of community and pride, a feeling of worth and strength. It was doing for others, standing up for a cause. Now they saw that it was what nurses and other women had needed all along. They entered the ranks proudly.

*　*　*　*　*

As the winter finally edged toward spring, Karon began to feel her spirits lift. In the previous months she'd faced more trauma than she'd ever have thought one person could cope with. First, the dismissal and the ensuing struggles with the bureaucratic red tape and governmental mumbo jumbo. Then in rapid succession her brother Brad broke a leg, her mother had to have a breast biopsy for cancer (it proved negative), her grandmother was diagnosed as having cancer, her middle brother John was temporarily paralyzed by a mysterious virus, and her brother Ron, who lived in California, was badly injured in an accident. "That's it," she told Joy one day as they sat in their office watching falling snow turn to rain. "I've been through the pits and I'm coming out."

Karon knew that for hours and days at a time, Joy had been left with the burden of the business. Now they'd be back together again. Karon's mind and energy were freed for the work that had to be done. No more family problems, she promised herself. No more time hassling with the hospital and the Illinois State Compensation Bureau over her unemployment benefits; she'd won the right to the money. (Both Karon and Joy had applied for the funds after being fired, but only Karon's claim was contested. They didn't know why.) True, they still had to spend a half a day each week waiting in line at the local compensation office and they resented losing the time, but they needed and felt entitled to the money, which was going to run out soon anyway.

"Oh, Joy, who ever would have thought running a business was so damned complicated," Karon mused as they turned from the window and the changing weather and looked at their books and records piled high on their desks. They were learning, Joy pointed out, though the hard way for sure. "We have to have a higher markup," she said. "Look at this, it's crazy." What she was pointing to was the file for the National Tea construction site project. "Our profit margin was almost nonexistent."

But how, they wondered, were they supposed to have known what it should have been? At the time they established the rates, the figures seemed reasonable. Stella and Marge, the nurses they had contracted for the work, were paid $40 for each day they worked. But Registered Professional Nurses only billed National Tea $48 per day. The difference hardly paid for their consulting time, the time and gasoline used driving out to the site for occasional spot checks, and the time spent on the phone with Stella and Marge who, after three weeks on the job, demanded contract raises and who increasingly began to look on the project as their own, rather than one established through the independent practitioners. Karon and Joy shook their heads sadly over the file. What could they do now?

About as much as they could over another incident, one with a drug salesman. In their younger, more naive, days Karon and Joy used to chatter freely about new ideas and plans. Once they told a drug sales representative that they hoped to set up a health screening program at a large urban shopping center. As they saw it, the center would give them space and publicity and they would offer blood pressure and diabetes testing to patrons for a nominal fee. The center would take a percentage of the profit and the rest would go to Registered Professional Nurses. Considering that thousands of shoppers visited the location every day, Joy and Karon were sure this would be a good money-making venture.

Apparently, the drug salesman agreed because he went back to his own bosses and sold them on the idea. The drug company applied for and received a hefty government grant to set up a similar screening program, then called the Illinois Nurses Association and asked for volunteer nurses to perform the tests. When Karon found out, she was livid and tried to discourage the INA from going through with the arrangement. After a while her phone calls were no longer returned.

They had been, in their own words, stupid about so much of the business end of their practice. Innocents in a land of sharks. Nurses with the image of Florence Nightingale still dancing somewhere in the reaches of their minds, with the words of the famous pledge playing in their hearts: "To practice my profession faithfully . . . to do all in my power to maintain and elevate the standard of my profession . . . with loyalty . . . devote myself to the welfare of those committed to my care." You don't bother with the crasser realities like money when you're being noble.

Karon and Joy hadn't even thought seriously about money when they had begun; they assumed it was one of those things that would work itself out. The harsh truth hit home when they were forced, finally, to up their charges for home visits and did so grudgingly, arguing with their accountant that most sick people couldn't afford to pay much for care. "But you can't give them care unless you're in business, and at the rates you've been charging, that won't last for long." Looking back, they agreed he had been right.

When Karon and Joy first began their independent practice, their basic fee for a home visit was $10—Sundays, holidays, morning or night, that's all they charged. For other services their markup was $2, much too low, they realized eventually.

That afternoon, they turned to analyzing their nursing techniques.

142

"We're losing money by going out in pairs," Karon pointed out.

"But it makes for better nursing," Joy countered.

"Maybe we shouldn't do tub baths; bed baths go more quickly."

"Tub baths are better for the patients."

"We spend too much time talking to some of the patients."

"Some of them have no one else to talk to."

"We do too many freebies."

"They're good promotion."

"We don't have enough heads or arms or legs to get done everything that has to be done."

"True." Joy said. "Karon, you'd only be happy with a thirty-five hour day."

Businesses need managers, promoters, and workers, they agreed. They were trying to be all these things and having a terrible time doing it. They also agreed that workers would be easiest to get, and decided to use other nurses more, to expand into areas that would suit this type of arrangement. More and more, they would try to limit themselves to the initial visit on home cases, then send other RN's for the follow-up. Office visits would remain their domain entirely, but they considered the advisability of limiting their hours. Meanwhile, there'd be more letters sent out to area companies trying to solicit business and more brainstorming about uninvestigated avenues.

Karon developed a plan for using registered nurses on senior citizen cruises and excursions. She made Joy write letters to American Express, Carte Blanche, and every large travel agency in the city, explaining her idea, but the responses were all negative. Then Karon suggested to the Gingess Formalwear company—suppliers of rental tuxedos for weddings—that along with the free glassware, newspaper subscriptions, and toiletries they offered to potential customers, they also offer, as a premium, complimentary premarital blood tests, to be provided by Registered Professional Nurses. To the president of the McDonald's System, she proposed a community health screening project, co-sponsored with RPN and funded by the hamburger chain. Both

143

firms said no, although McDonald's advertising agency offered her a job.

Karon and Joy performed camp physicals, and taught first aid to Boy Scout troops, but their plan for providing emergency assistance to patrons and employees of local restaurants went nowhere. When Joy announced that they would offer an escort service for the handicapped and elderly, she received only one call, from a woman who two hours later cancelled the appointment. Another progressive idea lost to what—fear, perhaps, or inflexibility, or simple suspicion of something new.

The hospital firing had set Joy and Karon thinking. They realized they needed options. Occasionally, however, they grabbed at straws, like when they decided that security work was a logical extension to the nursing business. Why not cultivate a dual expertise as bodyguards and nurses? They were already trained in the latter; if they could qualify for the former then they could offer a unique and hopefully profitable service, to augment their routine nursing practice. So for six Saturdays in a row, Joy and Karon attended a training course at a nearby junior college to earn the certificates that would allow them to perform security work and to carry weapons (which they never did).

Their first case came from Ralph who, as part of his own private detective work, was investigating a nurse alleged to have defrauded state agencies of thousands of dollars. Fifteen years before, this woman, Katherine K., had injured her ankle on the job in a small town in Wisconsin. Since then she'd been collecting workman's compensation and billing the state for prescriptions of Talwin, a synthetic narcotic pain reliever. After Katherine refused a settlement of $100,000 plus fully paid surgery by a top orthopedic surgeon, Wisconsin authorities became suspect. They were sure she was working despite her claims of full disability and they thought she might be selling her drugs illegally. The woman had recently moved to Chicago and the case had been turned over to Ralph's agency.

He had three clues: Katherine's name, a post office box number

144

where her checks were sent, and the name and address of the pharmacist who filled Katherine's prescriptions. "You girls want to try this one?" Ralph asked Karon and Joy. "I'll contract your business on a consulting basis and you see what you can do. With your uniforms you'll get into all kinds of places I'd never get to." That was Ralph's hunch and he was right. Within two weeks, Karon and Joy had sewn up the case.

First they called the Illinois Division of Nursing, Department of Registration and Education. Katherine was not listed, meaning she did not have a current license for practicing in the state (also meaning that if she were working her employer hadn't checked into her credentials or didn't care that she was not licensed). Next the two went to the pharmacist's shop but the only information they got led to a dead end. At the post office they encountered a scrupulous clerk who insisted the information they wanted was confidential. Karon handed the man one of her business cards and explained that Katherine was a nurse they needed to talk to about their practice. "I can't tell you why we have to find her, but I can assure you it's very urgent," she said.

Although Katherine had already moved from the address the postal clerk gave them, Karon was able to talk to one of the nurse's former neighbors. From her she learned that Katherine's husband operated a medical supply house featuring used equipment. Using their business as a cover, the nurses made an appointment to see Mr. K.

"Oh, yes, we're always looking for good buys," Karon said as she and Joy climbed a flight of dingy stairs in the shabby north side supply house owned by Mr. K. "We're in independent practice," she explained as they made their way through piles of discarded urinals and bedpans. "In fact, we're thinking of opening a second office, in this general area. If only we can find dependable nurses to help out."

Mr. K. took the bait, told them his wife was a nurse, and gave them the name of the hospital where she was employed.

Now all they had to do was find out which shift Katherine

worked and then witness her signing in for duty. For four nights they staked out her apartment, parking down the street and doing their surveillance through a pair of old opera glasses. Finally they saw Katherine emerge dressed in her uniform but they lost her in traffic on the way to the hospital and arrived too late to follow her in. The next night, though, Karon and Joy waited in the hospital lobby. When Katherine came in, Karon sweet-talked her way past the guard and tailed the other nurse upstairs where she clicked her miniature camera to get pictures of Katherine at the duty roster.

That night, Karon gave the film to Ralph who passed it along to the Wisconsin detective agency that had hired him for the job. Faced with the evidence Karon and Joy had obtained, Katherine agreed to a final settlement with the state, ending her career in deception.

Occasionally Karon and Joy received other calls as investigators but their security work would never amount to more than a diversion from their real business. They had a service to offer, they realized, and that was independent nursing. The challenge was in finding the need.

This time they turned their attention to nursing homes. Karon made a list of the centers in their area and wrote to each of them offering the services of Registered Professional Nurses on an hourly, daily, even weekly basis. The requests began almost immediately.

Prior to this Karon and Joy had only a passing acquaintance with nursing homes. They'd heard the horror stories and the tales out of school, some of which they believed, but many of which they greeted with skepticism. Only now would they see for themselves.

Most of their duty shifts were late evening or night to morning. The two women lost track of the times they found only a licensed practical nurse in charge, or were left with no physician's number to call in case of an emergency. Once Joy got a call from a high school girl who'd been the only person on duty the evening an old

146

man died. She'd been hysterical and frightened, ignorant of procedure and too upset to act at all, and Joy had had to arrange for the removal of the body. At another home a nurse showed Joy the empty rooms the aides used at night for sleeping with their boyfriends. Occasionally Joy would take a day shift when a last-minute call came in. Because she liked to keep busy, she would often help the aides and orderlies with bed changes and other chores. It was something to do and was a good way to get close to the patients. The other workers thought she was crazy. "Nobody does nothing but their own job around here," one woman told her.

As independent nurse practitioners, Karon and Joy were called in when help was short or absent, which was the case more often than not. One evening they walked into a five-story facility that housed 400 patients, 80 on each floor. Karon was assigned the top floor, Joy the second. Neither of the nurses had ever been in that particular nursing home before. They knew nothing about the physical layout or the patients, and had no idea who, if anyone, was in charge of the three other units. The day-shift people left keys to the medicine rooms, along with an emergency number, that was all. Karon and Joy could not leave their floors, but they did call each other periodically to check on progress, to hear another friendly voice. Both of them found conditions in the home deplorable, hall carpets that squished underfoot, the smell of urine heavy in the air, walls that needed paint, floors that needed cleaning.

Karon's shift went quietly, but Joy's did not. Between 8:00 and 10:00 P.M. three emergencies developed on the second floor. A stroke, convulsions, screams, and quiet prayers filled the night as Joy raced to phones and bedsides, desperately working to stabilize unstable conditions until hospital ambulances arrived. Three floors above, Karon paced angrily. She was trapped in her own responsibilities, unable to help her partner, waiting for the call that would tell her it was all over and calm again on two. "It was like going into an eighty-room hotel and being told I had eight hours to learn everyone's name and disposition by magic," Joy complained to Karon. "I couldn't be on call and read charts at the same time, but no one told me who to watch for."

Both women went home that night pale and tired, depressed by the events of the evening, convinced no one really cared what went on behind the impassive brick edifice of the convalescent home, swearing they'd never go back there again.

Another time when Joy worked the day shift at a different old people's residence, she had the opportunity to watch an exercise class in session. Thirty men and women, who looked ancient even though they might not have been, sat in a huge circle, wheelchairs and shaky folding chairs pulled close together. The scene angered Joy. She learned that the "therapist" was a 30-year-old housewife. "Do you know what those people did?" she asked Karon later. "First they stamped their feet up and down on the floor for five minutes, then they picked up their hands and flexed their fingers for another five minutes. That was the exercise session. I nearly cried watching. Maybe that's all some of them could do at this point—Lord knows how many years they'd done nothing but sit around and vegetate, but if they'd had decent care to begin with, they wouldn't be like that." And she talked about her idealized old folk's home with it's swimming pool and garden, the one no lending institution would help finance because Karon and Joy were "just nurses."

When one convalescent home advertised for charge nurses, Karon and Joy applied for the positions, hoping they could work out full- or part-time schedules that would coordinate with their business hours and would finally give them some say about the quality of care provided for the elderly.

"What exactly are the responsibilities for these jobs?" Karon asked.

"You do what's necessary," the administrator explained. "If the cook doesn't show up, you prepare the meals. If the matrons are absent, you clean the rooms. If another nurse doesn't come in for her shift, you have to take her place, so you'd be on call 24 hours a day."

The next morning Joy phoned the home and withdrew their

148

applications. "We wouldn't work there for thirty dollars an hour," she told the interviewer, thinking to herself that what he wanted was a couple of oxen, not two nurses.

Finally the ideal situation appeared. A physician had left the employ of a local convalescent home and the administrator asked Dr. Castro if he would assume responsibility for that doctor's patients. About ten people, all on public aid.

"If your business can help and do most of the work, we'll take this on together," John Castro said to Karon.

The next day the independent practitioners went to the home for a list of the patients involved. The facility was noticeably rundown and there were at least 25 names on the sheet they were given. Looks suspicious, Karon thought, but we can't give up now. Three nights later she and Joy returned to do their research, read charts, note medications currently prescribed, and talk to the patients and the aides on duty. The home, they discovered, had a tremendous staff turnover; it was, in fact, a training ground for foreign nurses who were hired as graduates and who invariably left as soon as they passed their state boards. "Order-A-Nurse," Karon and Joy called the operation. On their first visit, the nurses had seen only the public areas of the home. Now, walking through the patient floors, they saw the extent of the negligence. A constantly lengthening list of patients to be cared for was the final problem. When Karon and Joy left the premises after midnight—after completing only half their work—they had nearly 50 names in hand.

It nearly broke Karon's heart to do so, but the next day she called Dr. Castro and advised him to drop the project. "They're trying to give you too many patients; there's no guarantee of consistent care; and you'd be ultimately responsible." It was, he agreed, a bad deal, in exchange for which he'd be expected to attend a luncheon meeting once a week and would be paid (if he could collect it) $7 per patient visit—out of which he, in turn, would pay Karon and Joy for their work.

Now, when calls from nursing homes came in, the independent practitioners tended to subcontract the work out to one or more of the ten nurses they had on call. Karon and Joy had seen enough; they'd still help out when needed, but they turned their energies back to their own patients.

One of the first waiting for them was a nervous, overweight 44-year-old woman who walked through the door carrying an array of papers and pamphlets.

"I have kidney disease and high blood pressure. I've had a heart attack and I'm diabetic too." She spoke quietly, her voice trembling. "Look, look at this. Eleven diets they have me on now. I'm so confused and afraid I don't know what to eat." She admitted, after much questioning, that she was sure she was dying ("No one will say it, but I know."), and that she was so lost in the labyrinth of instructions of what she could and could not eat that she'd taken to living on water, which she would boil for herself, one cup at a time.

It was a slow afternoon, so Karon and Joy went to work. They shoved aside all the patient's diets, then on a clean sheet of paper made her write down all the foods she'd eaten regularly in the past or would like to have eaten if she thought she could. Next they dragged their two nutrition books off the shelf and looked up the foods on the list, calculating their nutrient values, then adding, subtracting, and figuring out what portions of each would give the woman the right amount of minerals, carbohydrates, and so on that she needed. Four hours later they had a simple, easy-to-follow diet typed out on two sheets of paper.

Karon had also found a copy of a Campbell Soup brochure describing a variety of special, single-serving soups for people on restricted diets. "We'll order some of them for you if you would like," she told the patient. The woman was delighted, said yes to the soup offer, and promised to check the food plan first with her doctor as they requested. At that point she probably would have paid the nurses anything they asked. All they charged was their routine fee: $15.

"We're crazy," Joy said after the woman left.

"Would you do it differently?" Karon asked, and Joy shook her head.

"We're just crazy, that's all."

The next time Joy and Karon saw the patient, her blood pressure was down, she'd lost weight, and she was smiling. "My doctor said he couldn't have done better himself when I showed him the diet," she said. "He's even gone on it himself." Then she picked up her boxes of soup, which the nurses had had delivered to their office, and left.

Karon and Joy felt so good about that particular patient, they were ready for the next obesity problem (it seemed the season). "His doctor won't put him on a diet," the mother whispered, glancing toward her huge, 16-year-old son who sat hunched in a corner, his face bent to hide the acne that had attacked in full force. "He says people know what to eat without being told and that all you have to do to lose weight is push yourself away from the table. But Tom's so embarrassed and I've tried everything. Now it seems all I do is nag and at school the other kids keep teasing him."

After checking with the physician and receiving a grudging okay to develop a diet for the boy, the nurses turned again to their nutrition references. This time they calculated calories, protein grams, and carbohydrates along with the nutrient content, keeping in mind the kind of food a high school sophomore might want to eat and would be exposed to at school or when out with his friends. An occasional hamburger without a bun and pizza without the crust, they agreed, couldn't hurt and psychologically would even help. The boy promised he'd try his new regimen— that's all the nurses could really ask—and the mother offered to try not to nag. Within days, it was really obvious the diet had caught on. The patient must have been following it religiously because every time he wanted something extra he'd call and ask permission, usually for a glass of milk. He lost weight and his acne began to clear. After a month, even his mother was on the diet.

Again Karon put her publicist's know-how into gear and tried to get Registered Professional Nurses on a nationally syndicated television show as guests. She received a polite no. As if in compensation, though, a national weekly newspaper ran a story

151

on their practice and Joy and Karon were swamped with letters from across the country. Nurses wrote: "I would like any information you have concerning a nurses' training program"; "Please send me any information useful in setting up an office such as yours"; "Would it be possible for you to give me some information about your business? . . . Just thinking about this makes me very excited and anxious to get started." The public wrote: "Congratulations, keep up the good work"; "We desperately need a service like yours in our community"; "Do you know of other nurses doing this type of work in this part of the country?"

Not all the results of the publicity were positive, however. Apparently, an official at the Illinois Department of Registration and Education read the article and was suspicious. ("Of what?" Karon asked.) There was a brief flurry of calls and visits and the agency finally decreed Joy and Karon must remove their signs from their car doors. The reason given: It was unethical for them to advertise. Although the nurses argued that the signs helped insure their safety in rough neighborhoods, the official would not be swayed.

All this time Karon and Joy had been operating their business, making house calls, doing office visits, contracting to nursing homes, filing legal complaints, standing in line for unemployment, and, as required by law, seeking full time employment. They'd not applied at any hospitals because they were afraid the incident at General would resurface. They did, on a whim, try for the Chicago Police Department and also answered ads in the Sunday paper for industrial nursing, an area they knew nothing about.

In June, the Fun City Amusement Park, a large recreational and shopping facility, advertised for a part-time nurse to establish a first aid station. Karon and Joy contracted for the job, working mostly weekends, long 12-hour days. The money was welcome since the nurses' unemployment benefits had run out by then and the change of scene was a psychological shot in the arm. They were working in a mad house, a fun house, surrounded by bright lights and laughter. No one was dying, no one needed a bath, no one had chronic complaints. There were lost children, pricked fingers, and occasional sprained ankle.

It seemed like fun and games, though eventually the thornier side would emerge. Here was a chance to mingle with people whose interest went beyond syringes and bedpans, an opportunity to meet famous singers and entertainers. It seemed a land of cotton candy. For twenty-four hours the two women laughed and joked about their good luck, about their turn in fortunes, about how easy it would be to work both the business and the amusement park. They drove home together the first two nights, ecstatic and planning, always planning for a bright future.

Then Karon walked in the front door of her apartment and the future fell in on her. The living room was strangely quiet and deserted, but in complete disarray, as if something fast and powerful had whirled through. Becky should have been home, but no sounds of TV or radio came from any of the rooms. Karon called out—no answer. She checked the bathroom—empty. She checked Becky's room. The girl was gone. Closets, drawers, shelves were cleaned out. My God, Karon thought, she has been kidnapped. Someone getting back at Ralph. You always heard about these things. A policeman sends someone up and then the person later seeks revenge.

For a few minutes Karon stood transfixed. She was suspended between fear and horror, between the awful present and the unknown future. The word *message* seeped into her brain and slowly she began looking for the ransom note, stumbling back through the apartment trying to retrace her exact steps. What is going on, what is going on? The question raced through her mind like a thunderclap; then she heard the front door. Ralph was home from work. Somehow, as he came through the door, Karon found the words to tell him what had happened. But he didn't think Becky had been kidnapped. No, not at all. Ralph was sure his ex-wife had come for her. And slowly it sank into Karon's mind. Yes, there had been problems lately. Becky's best friend had moved away and she'd begun hanging out by the pool with an older crowd. Karon didn't approve and told her so. She also imposed stricter study hours, which the 14-year-old had started to balk at. But none of that was serious, Karon thought. None of it could have led to this.

Ralph called the police. He reported his daughter missing. When the squad car arrived, he and Karon were talking to the janitor who claimed he had seen Becky walk out with a woman. "Do you know where the girl's mother lives?" the investigating officer asked. No, they didn't. A description of the girl went out over the wires and all night, while Ralph brooded, Karon racked her brain, trying to think of someone who might know where the woman lived. By morning, she remembered a distant relation and made the call that proved helpful. Ralph's ex-wife had been seen just the day before, getting off a bus on the corner of 99th and Bacon, had been seen walking into a complex of apartments just 100 feet from the bus stop. Ralph called the police again; then he and Karon drove to meet them at the spot they thought they might find Becky.

The girl wasn't home. Neither was Ralph's ex-wife, but a few minutes later Ralph spotted his daughter in a nearby schoolyard. Becky had nothing to say to Karon and little to say to her father. She'd changed her mind, that was all; she wanted to live with her mother again.

"You know, it's up to you," Karon told Ralph on their ride back. "I'll do whatever you want."

He waited a long time before answering. "I want her back. I want to fight to get her back."

"Okay, then that's what we'll do."

Every night thereafter Karon went to sleep watching her husband, wondering about the confusion and the deep sorrow she knew he was experiencing; every night she watched a bleak future descend closer. Every day Joy watched her friend, wondering what was next, wondering if there was any justice in the world, any god in the heavens.

154

chapter ten

*T*hank God for Fun City, Joy thought, as she and Karon drove home after another rowdy weekend's work at the family recreation center. Imagine, an amusement park keeping you sane! So often now, the two nurses sat in their office staring at the phone, wondering what the next call would bring. Another question from the EEOC investigator about their sex discrimination suit. (He kept asking them questions but had no answers for any of theirs, and it was now nearly a year since the inquiry had begun. "How long does it take?" they implored, but he brusquely waved them away, assuring them only that they'd be the first to know when a decision had been made.) Or maybe the next call would be Karon and Ralph's lawyer with news about Becky's custody case, which also was promising to drag on indefinitely.

"Oh, please, let it be Fun City," they'd silently cry when the phone would jingle finally. Not a rectal abcess—they'd had one of those recently, a painful sight. Not another foot fungus or head full of lice. Just a pleasant, simple call saying they'd be needed extra hours at the Fun City first aid station that weekend and could they come in?

But even in the land of Oz, dark clouds would roll across the sun. All gaity was forgotten in the hysterical vomiting of a frightened child or the gasps of an asthmatic woman. If patients could not be moved to the first aid office, the nurses went to them, usually running with black bags in hand. Most injuries were minor; most illness resulted from too much cotton candy mixed with too many rides. You never knew, though, what you'd find waiting around the corner.

One day they got a call about a man who was having difficulty breathing. Karon and Joy found him wearing his bus driver's uniform and standing next to a yellow school bus in the parking lot. He was trying to lean against the vehicle but kept sliding slowly into the open space before him. Nearby stood the chaperone and a group of 40 frightened youngsters, including the driver's own ten-year-old son. The situation looked serious and immediately Karon called for paramedics from the local hospital, while Joy helped ease the man onto the blanket she'd spread on the ground.

In minutes the rescue unit was on the scene. "Get that damned kid out of here," one of the men yelled at Joy, while the other shoved Karon aside and began checking the victim's vital signs. "We've done that already—here are the results," Karon said. "Hook him up and get the hospital on the radio." The paramedic, a young man, didn't even look at her. "We've got our procedures, lady," he said. "Don't you have something else to do?"

Infuriated, Karon stepped back because she didn't want to argue with him in public. She and Joy stood on the sidelines and watched as the two men wasted precious minutes doing what the two nurses had just done. They stood and watched as, finally, the victim was placed on a stretcher, rolled into the back of the ambulance truck, and connected to the telemetry system that relayed important bodily function information back to the emergency room, where a nurse or a doctor would review it and transmit orders. They stood and listened as a voice crackling over the airwaves directed the men to start up a "D-5-W IV" (sugar water), and then they stood for 20 minutes and watched as the one paramedic poked and probed, trying to find the magic connection between the needle and vein. Perhaps the rescuer had too little experience in the procedure or perhaps, because the victim was black, the medic could not readily see the vein.

"You're supposed to *feel* it!" Karon whispered to him. She was kneeling on the front of the ambulance now trying to convince the young man to let Joy insert the IV. "She's been doing it for years

156

and if there's no problem with your policies or whatever, why not let her do it?" Karon kept saying, and finally she won out. The paramedic backed away and let Joy slip in to finish the job.

"No, no, not there," he said, as Joy reached for the vein in the bend of the elbow. "The doctor always makes us put it in the hand."

"Well, you pick it and I'll stick it," Joy said.

Then, within minutes, the patient was on his way to the hospital.

"He suffered a coronary, but he's okay now," Karon called out later in the first aid station after checking with the ER. "Imagine that group leader wanting him to drive the bus back first."

The more Karon and Joy worked at the Fun City amusement center the more they saw paramedic teams in action. "I'd take the old fireman-ambulance drivers any day," Karon said one morning. "They would transport immediately." She and Joy had just watched a young paramedic perform a vaginal exam on a woman three months pregnant who'd started to bleed during a walk through the park. They conducted the exam in the rear of the rescue truck with the back door open and a full squadron of spectators gathered around. Audience chasers, Joy called the men.

At least no one was placed in great danger because of the situation. Not like the woman with the ice pick wound in her chest. "I don't believe this," Karon thought, as she ran toward the main entrance of the park. This is supposed to be a fun place. The call had just come in: a woman had been stabbed; she had collapsed by the front gate. Emergency. Apparently, the victim was bringing her son to the park that day and her ex-husband, upset by the recent divorce, followed them in his own car. He'd parked near the entrance and when they walked up, he leapt from the auto, ran over, and plunged the pick into the woman's chest, possibly piercing her heart or lung. Karon had a cellophane pressure pack secured over the wound when the paramedics drove up. "Hook up the EKG, keep the oxygen going, and transmit," she shouted to them, but the men were more concerned with removing the pack and re-examining the victim. "Don't touch that—her lung might collapse," but they ignored Karon's warning.

Minutes later, however, after radioing the hospital the paramedics found themselves doing exactly what Karon had said, this time on doctor's orders. They replaced the pressure pack, they started the EKG, and they transmitted, but they didn't say a word to Karon. Incredibly, once the patient reached the hospital she was x-rayed and told she could go back to the park; she appeared to be fine. Unfortunately, the diagnosis had been made from a wet x-ray, which can be misread. Later that night when the radiologist routinely rechecked the dry x-ray, he discovered that the patient did have a collapsed lung. The hospital immediately called the woman at home and urged her to go to the nearest emergency room as fast as possible. The woman spent three days in the intensive care unit and recovered fully.

This is almost like the hospital all over again, Karon realized. The nurse does the drudge work and the men move in for the glory. Karon had known, when the deal with the amusement park was made, that she'd be involved with these rescue teams. She'd been looking forward to it. The equipment they brought to the scene was beautiful; the opportunity to communicate directly to the hospital—instantly relaying vital information—could save lives. Karon had expected to work with these people (she did have more medical education and clinical experience than they did), not be shoved aside, demeaned, and ignored. "What do you think of paramedics?" she asked Dr. Castro once on a return ride from a joint home visit. He merely raised his eyes. "Remember," he said, "it takes longer to make a baby than to make a paramedic."

*　　*　　*　　*　　*

From a celebration of life to an abortion clinic; that's where the independent practitioners moved next. Two days a week a local doctor turned over his offices to the business of aborting un-

158

wanted, unplanned, unborn children. He himself did none of the work involved. He didn't approve, he said, but this was the world today. He simply collected a share of the money and let several other surgeons handle the actual abortions. All of the men were staff doctors at nearby religiously affiliated hospitals where abortions were not performed, but none seemed to have qualms about working at the clinic.

Karon and Joy shied away from nothing in their practice, but they discussed this move carefully before committing Registered Professional Nurses to an agreement with an abortion clinic. Neither of them believed in abortion but neither did they believe in the kind of hypocrisy they'd seen throughout the years. They both knew Catholic nurses who condemned abortions for other women but had had one themselves. They also both remembered the days when abortions were illegal except for "therapeutic" reasons, and women were brought to hospitals bleeding from knitting needles inserted in their vaginas to induce miscarriage, or were admitted to psych wards as the first step in gaining approval for a legal abortion. Finally, Karon and Joy decided that while it was not their place to judge the actions of others, it was their job to provide medical care to those who needed it. "We don't approve of shooting," Karon argued, "but we treat people who are shot." So every Wednesday and Saturday afternoon the nurses went to the clinic or asked one of their associate nurses to work there.

The offices were pleasant to work in, though an incongruous setting for the work being done. On all the walls, in the waiting room and the patient rooms, hung pictures of clowns—bright, cheerful pictures of smiling faces and laughing eyes. Joy groaned when she saw them. "How can these women sit here?" she wondered. She also wondered who these women were. Before, the abortion clients they'd seen at hospitals tended to fall into two categories: stewardesses and middle-class, white, teenage girls. Now with the force of the law behind them, who would come through the door?

Joy soon found out. The patient was Every Woman: she was the mother down the street having an abortion because she wanted to spare her husband ("We've got five kids now and he's working too hard; another one would kill him"). She was the woman at the supermarket pregnant, not from her husband who'd had a vasectomy, but from her boyfriend who hadn't. She was the widowed secretary who'd been raped by a teenage gang on Christmas Eve. She was young and white and most often there alone, or she was young and black and accompanied by her mother.

The first Christmas Eve Joy and Karon had to work at the abortion clinic, four patients showed up. Another day a woman came to the center in a slim-fitted evening dress and short rabbit fur jacket. She had an abortion, listened to the obligatory lecture on birth control, drank the obligatory glass of pop, ate the obligatory cookies, and walked off to attend a wedding. Another patient was a bride-to-be who wanted an abortion because she was worried if she were pregnant, her wedding dress would not fit properly, which would "ruin the wedding." One woman had been using birth control pills until, at age 23, she suffered a stroke and temporarily lost her ability to speak. Following that experience she wouldn't try even an IUD and now, with a noticeable limp in her left leg, she came to the clinic, pregnant and alone.

Some of the patients had had abortions before (one held the record for three previous visits); these women tended to be blasé. Some were guilt ridden and close to desperation. Some were hostile, resentful of the clinic staff there to help them; they seemed to act as if the aides and nurses were somehow responsible for their predicament. Others swore they'd kill their partners or else never have sex again. Most of them, however, had little to say. "The doctor yelled at me to shut up and lie still," was the most common complaint the nurses heard, but this one they did not try to counter. "That's legitimate," they said. "If you move there's danger of puncturing the uterus." And one patient raged that the doctor who worked on her "wrote on his pants." She was right; he was marking his operations one by one on his pants leg so as not to lose track of the number of patients he'd handled that day

The clinic functioned like an assembly line, but the clients seemed to want things that way. Few really cared to talk or be counseled afterward (no professional pre-abortion counseling was provided, the theory being that the women had already made up their minds or they wouldn't be here). As a rule, the patients came in, completed the requisite forms, answered the standard questions, then waited—six or seven of them at a time in the same clown-infested room, each aware that she knew exactly the secret the others would take with them when they left. For few of the women who came to the clinic came with their real names. Abortion may have been made legal, but it was still far from holy.

Almost invariably a small group of Right to Life advocates gathered outside the clinic when it was open. Standing on the public sidewalk that led to the front door, they passed out anti-abortion literature and tried to talk to the arriving patients. Most of the women ignored the protesters but some would come into the clinic distraught by the encounter. One patient was so upset she could not go through with her surgery, though she did return a week later.

Joy and Karon believed the patients had a right to the abortions they sought, but the nurses sometimes heard tales that bothered them—like the time a hysterical woman thought she saw a baby's arm fall to the floor during her abortion. On some occasions women who may not have been pregnant were given menstrual extractions. Karon and Joy looked at the records and shook their heads. Who was at fault, the patients who insisted because they wanted to be "sure" or the doctor who went along with the requests? One time the doctor who operated the clinic turned away a young woman who was five dollars short of the $167 abortion fee. He said it would teach her a lesson to have to make the 95-mile round trip again to her home in a small Illinois town to get the additional money.

The average time for an abortion at the clinic was about nine minutes, so as not to prolong the patients' discomfort. (After a Chicago newspaper published a major exposé on downtown abortion clinics, the time per surgery at the local clinic zoomed up to 15 minutes per abortion, and for a two-week period the surgeons actually came into the recovery room and checked on each patient, reminding them that abortion was not, and should not be used as, a form of birth control.) Once an abortion lasted an hour. Outside the operating room, the staff could hear screams and moans and the sounds of drawers being opened and slammed shut. The patient was in hysterics, the doctor was shouting, and Karon and Joy waited to be called in, but they never were. They'd been brought in to deal with the postsurgical procedures and that's all they were ever allowed to do. Check vital signs, pass out juice and cookies, watch for problems, and give pep talks on birth control.

The nurses were constantly surprised by the lack of basic knowledge many of the patients displayed. Some simply knew nothing about their bodily functions or methods of preventing conception. When Joy, in the standard post-abortion talk session, gave one woman her month's supply of birth control pills and told her how often to take them, the woman asked where they went. "What do you mean?" Joy asked, completely puzzled. "You know," the patient said pointing to her pelvic area. "Do they go in here? In the vagina?"

Another client came back for a four-week checkup—almost none of the patients ever did and since most used false names it was impossible to follow up and determine if they'd seen their private physicians—and she complained that the vaginal suppositories she'd been given for an infection hadn't worked. Karon went over the instructions with the woman and about the third time around discovered the problem: the patient had been eating the waxy little things, foil wrapper and all.

One day a woman sat in the recovery room mumbling over and over that she couldn't believe that she had gotten pregnant. "It's impossible," she said to Karon.

"Well, what kind of birth control were you using?" the nurse asked.

162

"Oh, none of that stuff," the patient replied. "But I was breast-feeding my son and I know you're not supposed to be able to conceive while you're nursing."

Karon questioned the woman further and learned she'd been breastfeeding the child for four and a half years. "He needs the warmth," the woman said.

For $200, more or less, any woman could come to the clinic and be relieved of her fetal burden. At times it seemed a cruel and heartless business. But from what Joy and Karon heard, the women received better care here than at the big clinics downtown, and those who had been through illegal abortion mills always commented on how much better this was.

Every time Karon and Joy thought of leaving the clinic and severing Registered Professional Nurses' contract with the doctor, they remembered the story they'd been told—by another physician—about the "good old days." Few doctors then would hazard such work and the women lucky enough to find an abortionist paid dearly. A Chicago doctor, an old black physician who'd practiced for years in the South, was considered among the most respectable and his fee was a minimum of $2,000. Other doctors often made referrals to him. They felt he'd paid his dues in his earlier years, working for almost nothing in a part of the country that, at the time, was extremely poor. They didn't resent his high cost—after all, he was risking his license every time he lifted the scalpel—and they knew he would treat their patients well.

How many of the women we see here could afford those prices? they wondered. Probably very few. Karon and Joy tried to concern themselves only with the legality of the situation and decided so long as there was no danger to their professional standing, they should stay. Maybe their little lectures on birth control, given to each patient, would help someone. That's all they could ask.

* * * * *

At about this time Registered Professional Nurses lined up

another good deal. This one was for a big floral show at McCormick Place, Chicago's convention center, which sits on the lakefront like a flattened and blackened spaceship. Too busy themselves and feeling magnanimous, Joy and Karon called two other nurses who d recently gone the independent route. ("We've got to help each other out," they said, extending the subcontracting invitation to the other two women.) The arrangement seemed amicable enough and no problems developed, until Karon learned that the other two had presented themselves at the center as the owners and operators of the business that had contracted the deal. "The backstabbing continues," Karon said, slamming the door on her way out to cool off. She and Joy had hoped for a pleasant relationship with the other two nurses; now that seemed impossible.

But at least some good had come of the incident; Joy was on contract part-time at McCormick Place, working in the first aid station. She was busy, so much so that at times when she came to the expressway she didn't know which way to go. McCormick Place, she had thought, what could possibly happen there? Well, for one, elderly ladies attending a flower show could topple like dominoes on an ascending escalator, leaving one injured frightened woman and one irate show manager.

"Here, let's walk her out of here—get her to a back room," he insisted, elbowing his way over to Joy and the victim who was sitting on the floor. "I've called for a wheelchair, she may have a fractured ankle," Joy said, trying to block the patient. "Nonsense. There's no fracture," the manager said to Joy, whom he knew was a registered nurse. "Just come with me, dear," he said to the injured patron. "How do you know there's no fracture?" Joy wanted to shout at the top of her lungs after the retreating figures. She wanted to hear the question echo through the cavernous hall, and stop the show manager dead in his tracks. Instead, she merely repeated the question to herself, stooped to pick up her bag and pushed her way through the crowd, following her charge. Later Joy chastised the manager for his behavior. "From now on, leave the nursing to me and I'll leave the flowers to you," she said.

A few weeks later Joy was on duty during a hardware show. There was also a musical comedy in the center's theater that afternoon, so McCormick Place was again host to a mixed bag of guests: senior groups, teens, school groups, and leisure-suited sales types. At about two o'clock security got a call from one of the restaurants on the main floor lobby area. "There's a drunk girl running around here eating off people's plates." Three guards left to investigate. Then another call came in. Joy took that one. It was a woman concerned about her daughter. "I know she's there somewhere; could you find her? She's very excitable and she didn't take her medicine this morning. I'm rather worried." Joy wrote down the particulars—name, age, description—and assured the woman she'd try. "There must be 4,000 people here right now and I'm supposed to find an 'excitable' 29-year-old," she thought. Then the phone rang again. Security wanted Joy's help. "We've got a nude woman down near the restroom area, the same one from upstairs, we think. She's fighting everyone off." Even as Joy was taking that call, the outside line rang. The concerned mother was back. She was calmer this time and to the point. "Look, my daughter was raped at 13; she's suicidal, and she just got out of a psychiatric hospital. Without her medicine she might do something crazy." Joy ran to the downstairs restroom. She had a hunch that the nude woman and the suicidal rape victim might be one and the same.

Joy heard the ruckus before she saw it. "You guys want to screw me but you can't," a female voice screamed. "Get your dirty hands off me." Three guards had the woman pinned to the tile floor but she managed to kick and thrash. Joy leaped in, hoping the sight of another woman would reassure the victim. (It *is* her, Joy thought, playing the mother's description back through her mind.) "Bitch!" the voice yelled. "Get the bitch with the long hair out of here." Joy's psych experience took over, and within minutes she had the young woman subdued and covered with an arrangement of jackets and coats. The nurse talked the security people out of phoning

165

for the police and stayed by the victim's side until the ambulance arrived. Then she went upstairs to call the mother and tell her where she could get her daughter. "You know," Joy told Karon the next day, "they never found her clothes. No one can figure out what she did with them."

Despite their optimism and new ventures, this was a trying period for the two nurses. They showed up one evening at a local drug store and began setting up their table and equipment for a health screening operation when suddenly the pharmacist arrived and ordered them out. "Just who the hell do you think you are and what the hell do you think you're doing? Get that junk out of here," he bellowed at them in the back corner of the store. Karon bellowed back at him, stopping the man in midswing from sweeping their materials onto the floor. Then, quickly, while she had him at attention, she explained their program, adding that the store manager had given them permission weeks before for the screening. "Oh, well, that explains things," the pharmacist said. "But I'm afraid you'll still have to pack up and leave. The manager you talked to—he's been fired."

Speaking requests kept coming in from professional nurses' groups, but the glamor was wearing off. Karon, especially, was upset by what she saw as the motivation behind the requests. She began to tell her audiences exactly how she felt. "I was not invited here because I am a nurse," she'd say, "but because I am a businesswoman, in the business of selling nursing." To Joy, she would add, "Nursing still doesn't count for much by itself, even to other nurses."

By fall of 1976, the EEOC was still stringing Karon and Joy along. A full year and a half had passed since the start of the investigation into their charges against General. No progress to date, just a series of questions to be answered. Joy and Karon tried not to think about their situation vis à vis the hospital but every once in a while they received a reminder. A few months earlier, for example, Joy had been in McDonald's for lunch when she bumped into one of the nurses she and Karon had worked with on the psych ward. Joy said hi, and almost immediately the other woman began to cry. "I've felt so bad about what happened and I just meant to call and say something, but you know how it is." And while the nurse rattled off a list of personal catastrophes she'd had to face, Joy thought to herself, Sure, I know how it is—you didn't call because you were scared. You were scared just like the others who won't even be seen talking to us.

Years before a different Joy would have listened to the excuses and accepted them, probably even apologizing because *she* hadn't called first. But this was a new Joy. "I'm sorry, I have to get back to the office," she said, looking at her watch. "Goodbye." And she walked out the door, never looking back, leaving the former coworker to rationalize her guilt to an empty stage.

Incidents like that hurt, and reminded the two women they remained ostracized from many members of their profession.

"I wonder if they'll ever learn to stick together," Karon said one day. She was busy typing a letter to the head nurse at the first aid station of an amusement park in Orlando, Florida. Finally, she and Ralph were going on a vacation, one week off for some rest and relaxation. "As long as we're going to be there I should talk to this woman," Karon told Joy. "I think it would be fun and maybe I can learn something to put in practice at Fun City." In her note, Karon mentioned her position and the similarities of their jobs, and asked for an hour or so of the nurse's time. A week later she received confirmation for the meeting, but when Karon actually arrived at the center she never saw the nurse. "She's in consultation with our doctor all day, and can't be disturbed," the secretary said. No, no plans had been made for anyone else to give Karon a tour of their operation. Karon was furious. "A businessman would never do something like that to another businessman, but a nurse will do it to another nurse," she said to Ralph. "No courtesy, no consideration. I come halfway across the country, I have an appointment, and she has to chitchat with the doctor. No wonder we have no network; we undercut each other every opportunity."

One day that autumn Karon and Joy were returning from the far side of the city, where they'd gone to do four insurance physicals. Two had been uneventful, two had been entertaining. "I took that little pill in the bottle, hope it was for something useful," the first patient had said, throwing Karon and Joy into a panic. The tablet, which was placed in the urine specimen bottle, was poisonous; it was used simply to keep the specimen from going stale while it was in the mail to the laboratory. But the client had just been joking and the visit had ended routinely, not in an emergency dash to the nearest hospital to have his stomach pumped. "I'll go get the specimen now," the second patient, another man, had said. Karon, misunderstanding him, got up and followed the man into his bathroom. She thought he had the bottle ready and was simply going to hand it to her. She realized differently when with one hand on his belt buckle, he reached back with the other and almost closed the door on her foot. How embarrassing, thought Karon.

She and Joy were laughing about the incidents as they headed back through the city to their office.

"Don't take the expressway," Karon said. "Let's just drive through on 63rd Street and go through the park."

"You want to drive through this neighborhood?" Joy was puzzled. Sixty-third was the main artery through a predominantly black, lower income area. It was hardly the scenic route, and Joy was not entirely comfortable being there alone, even in the daytime.

"Need any gas?" Karon asked, keeping the conversation going.

"Gas? Even if I did, I wouldn't stop for it here. Karon, what's with you?"

Nothing was with her Karon said. Never mind. Just drive. A few minutes later the younger nurse started up again. They had another physical scheduled for later in the week in that area; maybe they should cruise around now and check on the address. They'd both attended nursing schools in ghetto areas and were careful now, always disconcerted by the lifestyles they saw. They just couldn't get used to the bars and steel gates they found drawn across the inside doors of people's apartments and they were still surprised too by how clean and neat so many of the apartments were in contrast to the condition of the hallways, the entrances, and the streets outside.

"Karon, are you nuts or something? I don't want to hang around any longer than we have to. We stick out like two sore thumbs here."

Just then Joy spotted a squad car behind them. "Oh no, he's motioning for me to pull over. What did I do now?"

Karon didn't answer. "Are we here for the reason I think we're here?" Joy demanded. Again Karon didn't answer, and Joy's heart sank. This is no accident, she thought, and that isn't just *any* cop in that car. "Were we out looking for Brian?" she asked Karon, but her partner remained mute.

Just then the police squad pulled up next to Joy's car. "Are you lost?" the police officer asked Joy through her open window.

"No, I used to live in this neighborhood and we were just driving by my old house. We're both nurses, out on an insurance physical."

"Do you still live in Chicago?" he asked, his question translating into, "Don't you know any better than to be wandering around here alone like this?"

"Karon, he doesn't know who we are," Joy said suddenly. It was only then, when Joy turned toward her partner, that Brian saw his former girlfriend hiding in the far corner of the front seat. Here he was, Brian, whom she hadn't thought about for years, who lately had been sneaking into her memory, smiling at her with those wonderful blue eyes, the ones she'd fallen in love with at 19, the ones that had looked at her innocently while the man behind them lied about his wife and child. He was divorced now, she knew, and recently she had been wondering how he was, what he looked like now, whether she could see him again and not be affected.

"Why don't we go for coffee?" Brian offered. He tried to look nonchalant and unaffected, but the expression of his face broadcast a mix of curiosity and smugness. The nurses demurred. "How about next week then?"

Karon made a split-second decision. "Sure, why not?" she said, mimicking Brian's attitude and being careful not to let her glance meet Joy's.

For the next seven days Karon would argue with herself. She wanted to see Brian; she didn't want to see him. Half her mind raged against such foolishness, but the other half quietly encouraged her. Life had been hell lately for her. The pride and purpose that had come from starting the independent practice had been squelched by the dismissal from the hospital. Frustration had replaced enthusiasm, and though she was determined to fight and win out in the end, Karon often found her spirits flagging. She needed an ego boost and didn't know where to find one.

Then the problems with Becky had started, and for a year now she and Ralph had been involved in the custody case, trying to retain legal right to the child. Although Karon attended the mandatory family counseling sessions and accompanied Ralph to the court sessions, she felt strangely disenfranchised. This was really a lawyers' battle; they ran the show and did the talking, and the primary actors were Ralph, his ex-wife, and his daughter. Karon was someone in the wings; she was not meant to participate as much as simply to look on while this drama of other people's lives unfolded before her.

Karon could not identify the feeling as such at the time, but she was jealous of these concerns in her husband's life. She felt left out, and for Karon, who liked to be in control, the result was depression. Then to top it all off, she had turned 30 and also, she decided, had started getting fat. The combination was too much. While on one level she continued her normal routines and projected the image of the older, wiser woman, on another level she yearned to have back what she had lost. Her youth. The carefree days of nursing school when, 19 and slender, she had ruled her own world. Time plays its tricks and so it did with memories of Brian. When she thought of him now, Karon did not remember the heartache and the lies; she recalled only the good times. Finding Brian again was not as important as recapturing what he and that time in her life represented.

Sitting in her partner's new Buick that afternoon, with Joy's curious and concerned eyes boring into her, Karon felt confused. What would she tell Joy? Karon only half understood her own motivations. Would Joy laugh at her? Would her friend be critical? Would she help? Or would Joy respond with what Karon had always said to her, "I'll never tell on you but I'll never help you either"? Karon would have died of embarrassment before admitting she had actually gone to look for Brian. Did that mean she had been using Joy as a ploy? After all, the two of them together had a legitimate reason for being here and could have just accidentally encountered her old boyfriend. Things like that happened all the time to other people, why not to her?

A week later the two women were again in the same neighborhood. Joy had reserved judgment on her friend, cautioning her only to do nothing foolish. Joy understood the turmoil Karon was facing and felt she had an obligation to stand by her friend. If Karon was determined to see Brian, then Joy knew Karon would see him. Better that she not do it alone. So when the nurses finished the scheduled insurance physical—listening to the now familiar excuses for the client's elevated blood pressure and walking out the door with the required urine specimen in hand—Joy said nothing as they drove to meet Brian for coffee.

From then on the foursome—Brian's partner was always along—met regularly. For coffee at McDonald's, for a Coke at the university hospital. Sometimes once a week, sometimes once a month, but always in a public spot. Karon's main worry was that they'd be seen and Ralph would find out. One day they were all having breakfast together when Bill, the nurses' phone man, walked into the restaurant. Karon wanted to hide but Joy eagerly waved Bill over and he sat with them for an hour telling his typical outrageous stories and thinking nothing unusual was at hand.

What ensued in the relationship between Karon and Brian was

171

a battle of egos. Brian would not believe he was merely a diversion for Karon, old "iron pants," as he reminded her she used to be called. He was waiting for a little action on the side. "Forget it," Karon told him. This had nothing to do with an illicit relationship. Maybe not, said Brian, playing it cool again, but people do develop emotional dependencies. "Maybe you will," he teased her. "And maybe one thing will lead to another."

"Never," Karon said, and she meant it.

As it turned out, the only person who ever fell for the beguiling sweet talk was Brian himself. After a few months of their adolescent rendezvousing, he had convinced himself Karon would leave Ralph for him. "You need me," he'd say, but Karon would only laugh.

For her, there was an unanticipated bonus to the relationship. True, the ego boost was undeniable and yes, she had recaptured some of the levity and joy of an earlier time, but there was more. This time she was in control of the situation; she was the married one who was using him. This was sweet revenge and Karon loved it. Her only guilt came from her feelings of hypocrisy. All her life Karon had condemned married women who became involved with other men. Now she was doing just that. Although her relationship was kept strictly on a nonphysical level, her guilt was nonetheless real.

"I know what I'm doing is not really wrong, but I don't think it's right either. It would hurt Ralph even though it doesn't have anything to do with him. This is just something I have to work out," Karon told Joy.

They'd had a long talk about Brian that morning. They discussed him on their way to a home visit, on their way back to the office, and again later over lunch.

"It's insane, really. When I'm with Ralph I never even think of Brian."

"Do you love him?"

Karon said no, but Joy was still worried. After all, Brian had been her friend's first love.

"You know if you leave Ralph, you leave everything," Joy went on. "Your family, your entire life, the practice, everything."

"But I'm not leaving Ralph," Karon protested, and in a way she meant that. She would never leave him for Brian. But she had thought of just leaving, going away to a new place where no one knew her name, where no one knew about Becky and the hospital, and where she'd never have to talk about that again.

"You're trying to escape from life," Joy said. "Maybe you can do that for a while, I don't know. But someday you'll have to come back and face it, even if you're a million miles away."

"I know," Karon said. Then that evening, with Ralph off on one of his hunting trips, she arrived at Joy's house with a basket of chicken for the kids. "So you won't have to make dinner," she explained. "We have work to do this evening, another appointment." Another meeting with Brian.

Joy uttered a few words of protest, but she went. "This is crazy," she thought, "Why am I chaperoning these two?" But she went, partly to ease Karon's mind and partly because she enjoyed the escapades. The rendezvous helped take Joy's mind off their fight with the hospital and distracted her from her own unexciting life. She and Gordon had pretty much gone their separate ways and Joy was finding the route rather lonesome. Brian was, she had to admit, an amusing person and so was his partner. Can't I have a little fun too? she thought. Can't I have an innocent conversation with a man? How many women, she wondered, still labored under the old myth that any dealings with men inevitably led to something else? The independent practice had taught Joy that life wasn't necessarily like that. And she had finally reached a point in her own existence where she could feel comfortable talking with men and would actually admit she enjoyed it. "It's dull talking just to women all the time," she told Karon once.

Still she wished this arrangement between Karon and Brian wasn't so surreptitious, even while the thought that she, Joy Smith Catterson, was leading a secret life amused her. At times the entire venture seemed like a lark and she and Karon like children. No one would understand, of course, but that's all it was, an intermission in their lives. If only Gordon did not find out; if only Karon would keep it sweet and innocent. There were nights Joy could not sleep for the worry, and others when, with a firm hold on the fantasy element, she drifted off amused like a child by a good story.

Joy still did not wear her wedding ring. Nor did she think she would ever put it on again. She had hoped that this action would evoke some change in Gordon, but that hadn't happened. Last year she and Karon had been invited to a dinner given by the insurance company for which they did the physicals. They'd gone only because they'd been promised an introduction to the audience, with a plug for their independent practice. They'd brought along their husbands because that seemed the respectable thing to do. Both men had had too much to drink—who could blame them, sitting there listening to the speaker drone on for three hours?—but Ralph had only been funny. Gordon had been embarrassing. "Is that SOB still talking?" he'd said at one point, so loudly Joy was sure half the auditorium heard.

It was to have been a wonderful evening: an introduction to a room full of businessmen, then a ride home in a limousine (their friends from the livery service had nothing scheduled that night and offered them full service for only $25). On the way to the restaurant later for coffee, Gordon had sat in the front seat with the driver.

"Where did you go when you dropped us off?" he asked, picking up the driver's hat and putting it on his own head, backwards.

"Home. I laid down and watched TV."

"You're lucky you didn't get kicked in the head," Gordon said seriously.

"Why? Did you get kicked in the head?"

Gordon looked at the man as if the driver had just asked the most ludicrous question imaginable. "No—I didn't get kicked in the head. Why would you ask a question like that?"

In the back seat Ralph and Karon were laughing, trying to get Joy to see the humor in the scene, but Joy could see nothing but her own anger. In the restaurant she pulled her husband to the side and pleaded with him, threatened him. At the table, when Gordon announced loudly that he thought the place was a real dump, Joy could only cry.

At some point after that incident—even Joy wasn't sure when—she decided she had to fight back. She was tired of being passive and, she figured, she had nothing to lose. Her life with Gordon couldn't be any worse. Maybe, just possibly, it could get better. But she didn't really care anymore. She just wanted to get even. At their next anniversary Gordon brought presents. Joy threw them away—flowers into the toilet and candy into the garbage. I am doing this, she said to herself, because these are gifts not from the Gordon I married, but from some drunk masquerading in his place.

Joy's *coup de grâce*, however, was the Irish Policeman's Ball. She made her plans carefully. She was, she told Karon, finally going to give Gordon a taste of his own medicine. Joy knew that the ball was important to Gordon; he was proud of his Irish heritage and there would be other, older policemen present whom Gordon respected and admired.

Even before the waitress came to the table where the Gibsons and the Cattersons sat with three other couples—all friends of Gordon's—Joy started. First she picked up the complimentary vial of perfume set before her plate and poured the entire contents down the front of her dress. (Didn't Gordon always manage something outrageous like that, spilling a drink or the creamer or the sugar bowl?) When Karon offered cigarettes around the table, Joy took one, though she had to turn her back on her husband before she could smoke it (Gordon hated women smoking.) When the waitress arrived, Joy and Karon both ordered drinks, amassing between them six pink ladies, which they stood in a neat row across the front of the table. One by one, they raised the glasses and emptied the contents in response to the series of toasts they

175

were offering. By the time the announcement came that dinner would be served soon and the bar temporarily closed in ten minutes, they'd finished all six drinks. "Gee, we're going to need more, aren't we?" Joy said to Karon. "I think I'd better take care of this." Without another word she walked to the bar where she purchased a tray full of drinks, all pink ladies. (Wasn't that Gordon's old trick, getting three or four bottles of beer to get him through these closed bar periods? How many weddings and dances had she seen that one at? All right, Gordon, she thought, this is for you.)

Meanwhile, of course, eyebrows were being raised and questionable glances tossed their way from across the table. Karon ignored the looks, as did Ralph, who was enjoying the show. As for Joy, she was simply determined to go through with the plan. She chattered nonstop to Karon and sweetly brushed aside Gordon's protests with repetitions of, "Now, now, dear. Don't worry about a thing." She could see he was angry and she thought, finally, it's your turn—see how you like it.

Gordon didn't like it. At the end of the meal, he walked out, embarrassed, furious, yet helpless in the face of his wife's insolence. Maybe that was the first dim light to penetrate. Maybe it was too uncomfortable to see a mirror raised to one's own self. Joy did not know how large a role that evening played in her husband's metamorphosis. Other factors contributed too. Hadn't he been upset when he finally saw a picture of himself taken at a friend's wedding. ("Am I really that fat?" he asked Joy. "I look terrible. I'm going on a diet.") Hadn't he been surprised at the skill and enthusiasm Joy demonstrated in the independent practice? He had taken this woman for granted and then found one day that he was forced to be proud of her. Maybe he'd been taking himself for granted too, and wanted to replace that complacency with a little pride.

Whatever, something happened and Gordon did begin to change. Not then, though. On that night there was a terrible argument in the parking lot, the bellows of the wounded male

176

humiliated by a woman; there was the long, silent drive home and the slamming of doors and the awkward exchanges the next morning as rage faded into confusion. Despite the hangover, a new experience for her, Joy got through the incident without once backing down, without ever succumbing to the temptation to apologize. She got through it on her own determination and with a little help from her friend.

I owe her, Joy thought, as she wheeled the car out of the garage and headed it into the city toward the meeting with Brian.

The independent practice provided the nurses perfect cover for their rendezvous. They were doing a large number of insurance physicals, as well as maintaining their schedule of home visits. Most of the home visits were centered in their own geographic area and occurred during the day, but the physicals took them throughout the city, at any hour of the day or evening.

The meetings with Brian went on for a little more than a year. They were Karon's lifeline through a stormy period; the more time that passed the more Karon gained control of her own situation and the less she needed this support system she'd created. Brian was very handsome, she had to admit, and he was witty as ever. But eventually, Karon began to see his shallowness and insincerity, and began to appreciate the depth and strength of the man she was married to. She had sought the carefreeness of her youth and slowly became burdened by the sense of foolishness that accompanied it. There was only one thing left for her to do—stop seeing Brian and tell Ralph all about it. Karon knew she had to tell him. The guilt would overwhelm her; she would always worry that he might find out from someone else and imagine something far worse had taken place.

She told him in December, 1977, after a Christmas party. She and Ralph had come in late after a lively evening with friends. Karon started talking around 2:00 A.M. and didn't finish until four in the morning. She hadn't bothered with preliminaries; what could she possibly have offered as a lead-in to this wretched story? She'd merely begun to pour her heart out. She was completely honest; gave Ralph dates, times, circumstances. She tried to explain why she had done it and why now she was through with the whole mess. And she told him that if he had found out and had told her to stop, she would have at any time, but how it was better and somehow necessary that she had worked it through on her own.

All the while Karon spoke, her voice oddly subdued, she was aware of Ralph's every move. How he alternately stared at her, then turned his eyes away to the floor. She watched him pour a double shot of Scotch over a jumble of ice, and somewhere in the back of her mind the fact registered that she had never seen her husband drink like that before. She saw him sit immobile, then get up and pace nervously, his face twitching, his right hand stroking his chin, stretching the flesh out of shape then releasing it again. Suddenly all the fun had evaporated from her harmless lark with Brian. She knew now that she had broken Ralph's heart and she was paying dearly for it with her own sorrow. He always told me I was one woman he could trust, she thought, and now I've ruined it, thrown it away.

Ralph said very little to Karon that night, except that he'd been nagged lately by the suspicion that something, he wasn't sure what, had been wrong. In the end, when she finished talking, he looked at her a good long while, then said he was tired and wanted to go to sleep. For the next few days Ralph was distant and withdrawn. He was on duty and gone eight to ten hours a day. Karon made a point of being home each day when he came back but she could think of nothing to do to penetrate his misery. Rather, she would just watch as he'd go to the bar and fix a drink for himself, once, twice, even three times in an evening, and she thought, My God, what have I done to him?

Later, Ralph told Karon she had no idea how close he'd come to leaving her, but he said little else about the incident. Eventually, when enough time had passed, he would tease her about it and eventually he had the last laugh. Ralph had heard Brian's name before but did not know him, although they were both policemen on the same force. When Brian was suspended and arrested for selling drugs—with his picture on the TV news and all—Ralph finally had a look at the man who for a short period had been his competition. "You really know how to pick them," he said to Karon, enjoying her discomfort, "a real softball you had there."

Joy was furious. "Do you realize what would have happened if we were with him when this happened? He was selling drugs—and we're nurses! People would have thought we were his suppliers. Think of the headlines: 'Nab cop, nurses in drug bust!' Fine friend you have, and I get dragged into it!"

For once Karon had no answers. She'd been wrong, terribly wrong about this man. Karon who believed in the rules, who wouldn't let a nurse have a glass of wine on Christmas Eve and who'd dragged a chaperone along on the only innocent fling she'd ever had, had been involved with a cop who sold drugs. She was glad he'd been there when she needed him, but she was finished with Brian finally. Later, when he was convicted and sentenced to prison, she would have sympathy for him but none for his situation. Brian was a dead end.

*   *   *   *   *

Even as the involvement with the romantic policeman was beginning to lose some of its appeal, the nurses' battle against the hospital was getting a welcome boost. In April, 1976, Karon and Joy received word from the Equal Employment Opportunity Commission that a decision had been made in their favor. The EEOC had determined, in fact, that their claim to sex discrimination at General Community Hospital could be substantiated.

Joy and Karon cried with relief. They went out to dinner, ordered wine, toasted themselves and all they'd been through. They talked about it all over again, releasing the pent-up tension of the past two and a half years.

"We did it," Karon said. "It's all over."

Except it wasn't all over. For days the two women waited for the next installment. They were sure there would be a formal meet-

179

ing, either at the hospital or at the federal building downtown, with the two of them, representatives from General, and an EEOC official. The official would serve notice to the hospital and detail the list of reparations to be made. Certainly, their records would be cleared; their seniority reinstated; they'd be given the references they'd earned in all those years of work and maybe, just possibly, they'd be offered their old jobs back. "I'd never go back to work there," Joy said. "Oh, I would, in a minute," Karon mused. They needn't have worried about what they would or would not do, because the EEOC never called back. After a week of theorizing and second guessing, Joy and Karon called their investigator. They reeled when they heard what he had to say.

"No, no. We don't do anything now," he said. "We just make the determination to see if there's a basis for a sex discrimination suit. We can't touch the hospital. That's your problem now. You have to decide whether to follow up with legal action. I mean, if you want to sue you can, and you can sue on the basis of sex discrimination, but that's up to you. We can't sue for you; we can't impose any fines or restrictions on the hospital; we have no legal redress with them at all."

The women had thought all along that the matter would end here. "We were led to believe that once the determination was made, that meant the matter was settled," Karon explained.

"Well, wherever you got that from, it's wrong," the investigator said. "We'll issue a Right to Sue notice—you get that after the official determination. Then it's up to you."

Karon and Joy didn't want it to be up to them, not just then. They were tired of the entire matter. They had poured an enormous amount of energy into getting this far. Look how many dead ends they'd followed up on on their own! How they'd had to argue with lawyers who tried to discourage them from ever going to the EEOC!

"When will we get this Right to Sue business?" Karon asked.

"I don't know." The investigator was kind but firm. He was already on a new case. Theirs would just have to go through the standard processes. Weeks, maybe months, would pass before the Right to Sue letter was issued. He had no way of pinning down the date any more accurately than that.

"Once you get the notice, you have ninety days to act; that's all I can tell you," he explained.

"In other words, we have to just sit here on the edges of our chairs ready to leap into action immediately, only we don't know when. We have to be in a state of readiness for some unknown period of time because that's the way things go."

"That's right."

"I'm sick of the whole thing." Joy nearly screamed as she lowered the extension phone to its cradle. "Sick of it, you hear?"

Yes, Karon heard and she was just as disgusted. She didn't want to talk about it, she said, not then. But how could they avoid discussing this new dilemma? Even when they tried to ignore the subject, their conversation invariably would come back to it.

"What good are the determination and the Right to Sue if we do nothing with them?" one would ask.

"They give us a sense of satisfaction, that we were right," the other would say.

"Is that enough?"

Sometimes the answer was yes, sometimes the answer was no. Then the arguments would take a new tack.

"How can we stop now, when we've come so far?"

"We can't. We shouldn't."

"But how do we go on? Where do we get the time, the money—surely it will cost money—the energy to keep going? This could take years."

And again they would turn away from the problem and immerse themselves in bandages and patients until they couldn't stand not talking about it.

Before, in their letters to the National Labor Relations Board, the Illinois Nurses Association, and the EEOC, the situation hadn't seemed as threatening as now. Suddenly, there was nothing between them and the hospital—no agencies, no fancy

181

officials, nothing to serve as a buffer. If the hospital had seemed an overwhelming foe before, how much more awesome now when they would be forced to face it alone? They'd thought the EEOC would do the wrist-slapping, but the agency only located the strap and then handed it to them. Eventually that summer Joy and Karon were forced to face the reality of the situation. They had until the Right to Sue notice arrived to decide: they could either drop the matter or pursue it. The only way of doing the latter was to sue the hospital.

"These are the choices, huh?" Joy asked over a late cup of coffee on a night they'd done five insurance physicals.

"Those are the choices," Karon replied.

"I don't want to go on, really, but I don't want to quit either. It's a matter of which I don't want more."

"I vote not to quit."

Joy pondered Karon's statement a long while. She knew that their decision would determine their course of action for the next months, maybe years. God, she was tired of this. But giving up now was like admitting you were wrong, wasn't it? Giving up now was the first step to giving up on things forever. You're a fighter or you're not. She'd only recently become one and enjoyed the feeling. Sitting in the quiet, half-deserted restaurant, Joy watched her life walk through her mind. She relived again the immense feelings of pride that had come with establishing the practice and all that went with it. Her real sense of identity as a person had sprung from that moment. Joy as daughter, as wife, as mother— these all played important roles in her life but Joy as a valuable person in her own right—that role now encompassed all the others. Somehow in her mind, to back away from this the ultimate confrontation prompted by the independent practice would be the same as deserting that new role. Joy looked at Karon over the formica table top.

"Okay," she said finally with a shake of her head and a grim smile on her face. "But how do you sue a hospital?"

"Damned if I know," Karon said. "But I have a suspicion we're about to find out."

chapter eleven

*I*n April, 1977, almost one year after they had received the EEOC determination, Karon and Joy closed the door to their office. They had no choice. For nearly twelve months, they'd watched as the free clinic down the street expanded and their own schedule of in-office patients dwindled. Already, the clinic had hired away one of the nurses RPN regularly subcontracted out to. Thanks to a large influx of government money, the clinic was buying medications in bulk and giving away free prescriptions. Worse, it had started doing its own lab work, which cut in tremendously on Joy and Karon's business. "Why should someone come here and pay us when they can go there for nothing?" Karon asked Joy. "We've been outmaneuvered." It had been months, in fact, since the two independent practitioners had received a single referral from the clinic, whereas in the past they might have had five patients a week sent to them from the community health service.

The decision to close the office was not an easy one. "Why don't you just look for a new location?" Ralph suggested one evening when he and the two nurses met for dinner. Karon shook her head. She was caught in a squeeze between the ongoing custody case and the pending lawsuit against the hospital, which might start at any moment. Then there were all their other patients to consider. How could they possibly maintain the home visits and the insurance physicals, relocate their office, repeat all the steps necessary to publicize their new office, and still fight the hospital? "We can't," Karon said, "unless we go goofy trying." This was, the women agreed, a time of establishing priorities. They were not as innocent as they had been before. Three years earlier, when they'd been fired from General, they'd blithely bounced off into the unfamiliar quagmire of legal protest, thinking the process would be a cinch. A few phone calls, a few letters, a few hours or days of their time and the matter would be settled. They had had a lot to learn, they'd discovered. They wouldn't make that mistake again. This was the final round in their bout to clear their names and professional reputations. If they lost, they'd have no recourse. So they wouldn't lose; it was as simple as that.

They were still independent practitioners; the base of operations was just going to be shifted for a while. Until they had a clearer picture of their future as nurses, they'd work out of Karon's home, still answering calls but doing all their work on location. "We'll be like movie stars; the world will be our set," Karon mused, the day their last in-office patient arrived. She was a middle-aged woman who came in complaining of extreme fatigue. "I feel like I've just had a six-month case of the flu," she said, "no energy, just blah. I can't do anything." She was worried because she'd already been out of work for months—"You can't waitress very good when you're worn out like this"—and because she had already been to a number of doctors in the city and had even been hospitalized at three different institutions. "I've had all the tests, but they can't find nothing wrong."

Karon and Joy talked to the woman for nearly two hours. They performed a routine physical examination and studied the list of the tests the patient said she'd had. "You know, there's one possibility," Karon said to Joy as they conferred in their private area behind the screen. "A latent infection of some sort that simply didn't show up on the other tests." Following standing orders, Joy took a blood sample and sent it to their lab, with a request for a differential on the white blood cells. Three days later they called the patient and informed her she had a simple infection. They also called Dr. Castro and made an appointment for him to treat the woman.

"I'm feeling so much better, thank you." The patient was back,

184

ten days after the start of her antibiotic treatment. She was smiling, had a new job lined up, and couldn't find enough words to express her appreciation. "Here, try these, they're delicious," she said instead and handed Karon and Joy each a box of candy. "Thank you again." And she was gone.

The door clicked shut behind the rejuvenated women and for a long time neither Karon nor Joy spoke. Each sat lost in her own thoughts, as the late afternoon sun brightened the orange glow of their draperies and made the floor beneath dazzle in the light. Finally, Karon got up and walked across the space from her desk to the door. How familiar the route had become. I could do this in my sleep, she thought, I could walk around the entire room with my eyes closed and not bump into anything. I could find the syringes and sphygmomanometers and stethoscopes without even looking. And if I force myself with all my willpower, I can even lock the door.

"Have some candy," she said to Joy, striding back on her return trip. "You'll need the energy."

All evening, the nurses packed, saying little to each other. The next morning they loaded their lawn furniture and two desks onto a rental truck and drove them to Karon's parents' house. They hauled their boxes of files to Joy's garage and their supplies and phone answering machine to Karon's spare bedroom, now an office. At the end of the day, after goodbyes and promises to keep in touch to the travel agent, the limo operators, the insurance agent, and the pharmacist, they each picked up their little black bags and walked away from four years of memories and hard work. "We'll be back," Karon promised, "don't you worry." Joy could only nod her head. She was too choked up to talk.

The two women had dinner together that evening, drinking a little too much wine and reminiscing endlessly.

"Any regrets?" Karon finally asked.

"No, just big plans for the future," Joy said trying to smile through the sadness she felt.

They drank another toast and went home.

* * * * *

If either Karon or Joy had been worried about not being kept busy once they'd closed the office, they needn't have bothered. The new Registered Professional Nurses phone jangled regularly. "Mother's feeling poorly today, can you come see her?" Hank Anderson would regularly ask. And the nurses would visit the 91-year-old woman and again remind the son that mother's lapses would not occur if he gave her the blood pressure medication regularly. It seemed that Hank was in the habit of witholding the medicine whenever he thought his mother "looked better."

Then Mrs. Garben called pleading with the nurses to visit her husband. "He's just had a stroke and I don't think he'll ever be the same. I'm so worried," she said. Karon and Joy arrived at the couple's modest brick bungalow that afternoon, prepared for the worst. They'd seen too many stroke victims debilitated, physically nearly destroyed. "Depending on how he is, we can recommend therapy," Joy said as they walked up the concrete path to the front door. "You'd think they would have told them that at the hospital." A pleasant, white-haired woman answered the door and led the nurses into the living room. The furniture was overstuffed and decorated with hand crocheted doilies. "Please, sit down," Mrs. Garben said as she settled into an armchair, tugging her skirt into place over her knees. The old woman smiled ruefully at them, shook her head, and began chatting half to them and half to the cat that rubbed up against her legs.

"Fred's having such a hard time of it. You know these things can be very serious, but of course you know that; how silly of me. Still, I can't help but wonder and think back on all the fun times we had together. We've been married 38 years now—that's a long time. Are you girls married, or is that kind of information confidential nowadays? Young people are so different from the way we were. Sometimes I'm afraid I just don't understand."

Joy and Karon couldn't figure out what was going on. Where was the patient? Mrs. Garben was asking them questions now

186

about how she could cope with Fred. Would it take long for him to regain his old strength? Was she being unreasonable to worry? "It would help if we could see Mr. Garben," Karon interjected, and the elderly woman became flustered, excused herself, and said of course. But then she started talking again. She and Fred had planned a vacation for later that year and she didn't know what to do about their plane reservations. She was asking Karon whether to keep on with the plans when Joy leaned forward to pet the cat that had rambled across the room to sniff at her white slacks.

"Who's that?" Joy asked suddenly. She'd caught a glimpse out of the corner of her eye of an old, white-haired man stepping lightly toward the mail box on the corner. He looked about the same age as Mrs. Garben. "Where?—here, let me put on my glasses." Mrs. Garben moved to the window and pulled back the white lace curtain. "Oh that, that's Fred. Mr. Garben, I mean. Look at the poor dear. He can hardly get around." Karon and Joy exchanged glances. What does she expect, a marathoner? thought Karon. He looks in better shape than any stroke victim I've ever seen.

Diplomatically, the nurses tried to tell the woman that, from all appearances, her fears were unwarranted. "We'll still be happy to do a brief checkup to report to your doctor," Karon explained, "but I really don't think your husband needs us. He's doing quite well, honestly." Mr. Garben agreed when he returned to the house, curious about the car parked out front. "Don't need no nurses," he said. "Healthy as a horse."

"They don't know how lucky they are," Joy said on their way back. "They really don't. What does she expect him to do, swing on the parallel bars?"

Ironically, Joy and Karon soon returned to General Community Hospital in a professional capacity. Karon's grandmother had been admitted six weeks earlier for cancer treatment and although Karon had visited her often, she'd not acted in a nursing capacity. "How are they taking care of you, Babi?" she'd ask, and her dying grandmother would reply that everything was just fine. Once,

187

however, the old woman did say how much she missed having a bath. "You mean you haven't had one since you were admitted?" Karon demanded. "Oh no, just the little sponge things, but I just thought that's all you get. There's no tub in the room, you know." But there is one down the hall, her granddaughter thought to herself. I can't believe it. Too lazy to give an old woman a bath. That afternoon Karon called her grandmother's doctor.

"Did you specify no tub baths?" she asked.

"No—never said a word."

"Do you object if I go in with my partner and give my grandmother a bath?"

"No. Go right ahead. I'll call in the morning and let them know private-duty people are coming on."

A feeling of déjà vu overwhelmed the two nurses as they made the familiar trip to the hospital. Aside from having to park in the visitor lot and being allowed to use the front entrance, everything was as if they had never left. "I feel as if I'm walking into my past," Karon said. "Do you think anyone will talk to us?" They were renegades returning on their own power, proud and determined, yet self-conscious and on guard. They could easily become maudlin, they knew, and wanted to protect against that, so Karon joked about being permitted to walk in through the front door, something they couldn't do when they worked at General.

Joy had been back at the hospital once before in an official capacity when, shortly after being fired, she had served as a private-duty nurse for one of their home patients who had had to be hospitalized. That had been a difficult experience in some ways but an easy one in others. She'd been alone, hadn't bumped into any nurse she'd known before, and had encountered enough hassles in caring for her patient to be sufficiently distracted. (Joy requested a food tray and blanket at 2:00 P.M.; finally, after lying to the nutrition department she got a tray at 6:00 P.M. The blanket never arrived and at 9:00 P.M., Joy made the rounds to the linen closets on the floor. When she found one unlocked she simply reached in and took what bedding her patient needed.)

This time was different, however. Karon and Joy were together as they'd been for all those years on the psych ward. This felt like old times.

"You know, in a way I hope we run into some of the people we knew. I'd like to see how they react," Joy said.

They found it strange to encounter the hospital staff from this new perspective. No cordiality, no assistance, only suspicion. The floor nurses eyed these two interlopers coldly, feigning indifference but watching every move Karon and Joy made. When the two independent practitioners wheeled their patient through the hall to the tub room a nurse was standing there, posted like a sentry. "It's broken," she said. "You can't use it." She tried to sound authoritative but succeeded only in being defensive. "How do you give baths?" Karon asked. "We don't," the other nurse replied and turned and walked away.

"Well I'll be a. . . ." Karon caught herself. "We'll show them. Joy get a sweater and blanket from my grandmother's room."

With the elderly woman properly bundled, the trio set off to the end of the ward, across a drafty corridor, and into the new wing, where an empty tub room sat waiting for them. "They still won't put out any extra effort, will they?" Karon later said to Joy. "I guess nothing really has changed much."

At their new in-home office, things hadn't changed much either. The calls kept coming in, some strange as ever. Karon answered the phone one morning to hear a hysterical woman on the other end claim she was having a heart attack.

"Where are you? I'll call an ambulance immediately."

The woman wouldn't give her address. She didn't like ambulances, she said.

"I'll send the police, they can come for you in a squad car. Lady, this is urgent if what you say is true."

When the caller said she didn't like police either, Karon began to get suspicious.

"How about the fire department?" she asked, now being just slightly sarcastic. "Do you think you like firemen?"

189

The woman hung up.

Later a young man called requesting a 24-hour private-duty nurse.

"Who is the patient?" Karon asked.

"Me."

"What is the problem? Why do you need a round-the-clock nurse?"

The caller explained that he was scheduled to have two teeth extracted and was terrified. He'd never had a tooth pulled and while he had to admit that his was a strange request for a 25-year-old man, he was serious. Reruns of Addison Clark played through Karon's mind as she listened to the explanation.

"Why don't we wait and see what happens?" she said finally. "If you find you really need a nurse, we'll accommodate you."

The man never called back.

One Saturday morning Joy returned a call from their message machine. She grimaced as she jotted down the particulars but agreed to schedule the appointment for 6:00 P.M. that evening as requested. "Brace yourself," she told Karon. "We have a fecal impaction."

Karon was angry, not simply over the nature of the procedure, which was bad enough (an enema was useless in dealing with an impaction; the only way to effectively remove the blockage was to don rubber gloves and literally chip it out), but also over the timing, which was worse.

"Ralph's cousin is getting married tonight. I told you we had a wedding."

"You'll just have to be late, that's all. It won't be the first time, that's for sure."

Promptly at five, the two nurses drove off, both in uniform, and Karon, with her hair done for a celebration, telling Joy the story of a medical student and nursing student who met over an impaction and were married soon after. Again, the nurses were prepared for a hushed, hurried reception and again they were surprised. A woman answered the door with a cheery welcome, escorted them in, introduced them to three other people in the living room, and asked if they'd like something to drink. The nurses requested diet soft drinks and sat with clinking glasses in hand wondering who the patient was. Surely not one of the people chatting to them about the weather and the traffic and the new shopping mall going up in the area. It was obvious there was a party going on. Rather insensitive, Karon thought, considering somewhere in the house somebody is suffering such pain. After about twenty minutes of nervous chitchat Karon turned to the hostess. "Excuse me, but where is the patient?"

"Patient? What patient?" Nobody here was sick. The woman looked at the two nurses as if they were crazy. "We got a call about a fecal impaction. I mean that's why we're here. We weren't invited to any party." One of the men roared, the other immediately thought this was a practical joke and tried to figure out who could have made the call. By the time he gave up—he decided he didn't know anyone who would know what a fecal impaction was—Karon, Joy, and the hostess were checking the address. No, they were not at the right place, but almost. This was 2218 West Algrove Avenue. What they wanted was 2218 West Algrove Place. "You'll find it, no problem, just remember a right, then two lefts," the cheery hostess said as she waved to them from the door.

Half an hour later, Karon and Joy finally arrived at the right house. They had driven circles through cul-de-sacs, been detoured around a series of one-way streets, had battled with a bee that had flown into the car and taken up a watch post on Karon's forehead, and had just missed having two motorcycle riders fly through their windshield. That happened when they stopped for gas, just as the biker and his girlfriend cut through the station, lost control of their vehicle on a small patch of oil by one of the pumps, and were thrown head first over the motorcycle and directly in front of the nurses' car. "What took you so long?" Ralph asked later at the wedding. "You wouldn't believe me if I told you," Karon said, surveying her wilting hair in the mirror. "But someday I will, anyway."

A week later Dr. Castro listened to the story and laughed. Things like that happened to him all the time, he said. "Makes life interesting." It was a damp rainy night and the three of them were traveling along a Chicago expressway heading out of the city to a far south suburb. Karon and Joy had received a call that afternoon from a man whose wife was seriously ill. The couple had no doctor and begged the nurses to come out. "I can't move her," the man said in response to all Karon's suggestions about getting the woman to a hospital. "You have to come." We also have to bring John along, Karon thought, after listening to the description of the patient's symptoms. She called the doctor's office immediately, got past his protective nurse/receptionist, and spoke to Dr. Castro. He agreed to go along ("I like house calls," he said over his nurse's protests), but only if they could make it late. He'd be busy until at least 10:00.

So here they were, totally lost, driving to a mystery trailer court none of them had ever heard of with a doctor so tired he was nearly punch-drunk lounging in the back seat issuing orders and talking out-loud to himself. "You know, all my doctor friends wonder where I go off with the two of you on these late-night excursions. They should know. I've even invited them along, but they're much too proper. They don't really believe we make house calls, but they can't take that chance either. Some of them think if they see a patient outside their offices they'll be turned into pillars of salt. Where the hell are we anyway?" They'd just driven past a mass of highway signs. "Hey, you said we were only going to 127th and already we're at 140th—what's going on?" Karon, the front seat passenger, waved him silent. "Have we ever deceived you before?" she asked. "Yes, but that's another story." Karon told John to go to sleep. "We'll wake you when we get there."

Joy looked at the clock on the dash. Midnight. She was just turning into the trailer park entrance, inching the car through the downpour. "Look for signs," she told Karon. "Look for numbers, anything. I don't know where to go." The park was nothing more than a maze inhabited with people and dogs. The people were mostly asleep and their tiny metal homes dark, but the dogs were up and barking. "Those dogs sound mean," Karon said. By now she and Joy were dashing around in the night, jackets held over their heads, trying to get close enough to the trailer doors to read the numbers. They'd had to abandon the car and the sleeping doctor after about ten futile minutes of driving the narrow, unlit lanes. They'd expected a yard light or some signal to direct them to the right trailer but so far nothing. "There it is," Joy said at last and she pointed across the way. "This one is 118, that has to be 120. There's a tiny light on in the front too."

Once they got inside and saw their new patient, any frustration faded. The woman sat in a faded armchair, her back and arms bolstered by an array of pillows, her head gently nodding down toward her chest. Her legs were so painfully swollen it didn't seem possible anyone's skin could stretch that far. The sores on her legs were hideous; they wondered how she could endure the pain. Every time the woman breathed, a raspy gurgling noise swept through the tiny living room and the husband, a wiry, nervous old man, watched with great concern and fear on his face. "She won't eat anything. She just sits there."

Ten years earlier the patient had been diagnosed as having congestive heart failure and diabetes. "I took her to the doctor for a while," the husband continued, "but it got to be so much trouble, she just wouldn't go anymore. So I did the best I could at home." While the man talked, Karon, Joy and Dr. Castro found their eyes wandering to the little table that sat to the patient's right. On it was an incredible heap of ointments, pills, and syrups. "Where'd you get these?" Dr. Castro asked as he moved across the room, his curiosity as well as concern taking over. "From the drug store," the man replied. "They got so many things, I thought some of them might help." The doctor shook his head. He'd never heard of half of these over-the-counter drugs. Some were obviously years old, their potency gone, others were simply innocuous compounds whose names sounded impressive but whose worth was nil. "You take all those things?" The patient forced a weak smile and tried to nod her head. "Yes," her husband said.

"Well, I've got to have her admitted to the hospital." The examination was completed and Dr. Castro had called the man over to stand by his wife. The words fell on the couple like a death sentence. They reached for each other's hands. They'd never been separated before, they explained, and with the husband's poor eyesight, well, he wouldn't be able to drive to see her except during the day. But if the doctor thought the hospital might help, then they would do it, that's all. If only she wouldn't hurt so much, maybe it would be worth the separation. Until then, until tomorrow, the patient wondered, would it be all right if she kept on with her old medicines? Dr. Castro looked at her a minute, then leaned over, and gently patted her arm. "Lady, if those medicines have kept you going for the last ten years, with those sores and that breathing, then you just take them for the rest of your life." (Which is exactly what she did when, two months later, she came home from the hospital, able to move around on her own power for the first time in years.)

It was 1:00 A.M. by the time the medical trio began wending its way back to the city, giddy with fatigue. Dr. Castro finally fell asleep in the back seat, but not before regaling the nurses with his plans for the three of them. "We'll hit every trailer court in the county. All we need is a CB—Karon, get a CB, put that on your Christmas list. Then we can be like the paramedics. We'll just radio in to the hospital: 'Castro and two nurses off to the next patient, off to serve the world.' We'll make a house call to Lake Geneva, to a wealthy millionaire. Then we'll stay to see if the medication works and we'll all have a short holiday."

About this time Joy, through Registered Professional Nurses, contracted for a position as an industrial nurse for a small electrical factory. Five days a week she was the medical staff for some 540 men and women who made sirens and signal wires. Joy enjoyed the people and the work, but she was constantly angered by the large number of employees who tried to claim fraudulent work injuries. "They must think I'm a real dummy," she told Karon, "or maybe this is accepted practice. I can't figure it out "

One woman, for example, called in sick with a "lump" in her

abdomen. "I think it's a hernia," she said. "I remember two days ago having to move a bunch of boxes and I'm sure that's what did it." Joy sent the woman to her doctor, who diagnosed the problem as an infection stemming from a Caesarean section scar. Every sprained ankle was work-related, from slipping on ice in the winter to slipping on packaging material in the warmer months. Every bruise seemed inevitably to lead back to work. The first day Joy saw one employee with a huge black and blue patch on her left calf, the woman had no idea how the injury had occurred. Two days later, during a routine followup, the patient remembered that she'd gotten hurt when she bumped her leg carrying a pile of baskets at work. "No, come on," Joy said. "If you honestly don't know how it happened, leave it at that. Why make something up?" The woman grinned sheepishly and agreed.

Because workers normally did not hesitate to come to the nurses' station for almost any reason (a first-aid visit was a bona fide excuse for leaving the work area and either cooling off or resting a while), Joy was especially suspicious of delayed injury reports. One time a man came in to complain of a sore back. "No Inglese," he replied to all of Joy's questions. He gave her a pantomime of a box falling on his shoulder. "You're sure this happened at work?" Joy asked. "You didn't fall down at home or hurt yourself at the company picnic?" "No Inglese," was his answer. The patient, still grimacing and hunched over, sat quietly while Joy completed forms and questionnaires for his file. Just then, one of the personnel officers came in to the room; he checked a few files with Joy, then repeated a joke he'd heard that morning at the local greasy spoon. The person who laughed the loudest was the man who spoke no English.

While Joy experienced this first-hand introduction to the world of industrial nursing, Karon continued her work at Fun City, where now she was in charge of first aid. Almost daily, her encounters grew more bizarre. People certainly do have strange ideas about nurses, she thought. One day, for example, Karon received a call from security about an urgent matter. Strange photos had been found taped to mirrors in the employees' rest rooms. They were allegedly pictures of employees shot from the neck down. All the subjects were completely nude.

"So what am I supposed to do?" Karon demanded.

"Well, we thought, being the nurse, you could identify the people in the photos and help get to the root of the problem," a nervous security manager said.

Karon looked at the man carefully. "You think that because I am the nurse I see everyone naked, is that it?"

The investigator was apologetic. The idea had seemed logical. Now, he admitted, it sounded rather ludicrous.

Another day, one of Karon's friends on the staff told of overhearing a park electrician berate the staff nurses to one of the female patrons. The patron had an injured hand, which Karon had taped. When the worker saw the bandage he told the woman that the nurses were unqualified and had no right to tape her finger. Karon listened to the story, then looked for the electrician, a young man about 25, who'd worked at the amusement center for about four months. She found him in a public walkway between two concession stands.

"I've heard what you've been saying about us and I would like to talk to you about it. Do you think we can go somewhere and discuss this?" Karon was hot, but tried to sit on her temper.

"Who do you think you are!" the man began yelling. "You're all unqualified, the whole bunch of you. Prancing around the customers, but you're never here when we work. Just a bunch of glory grabbers. You nurses don't know anything, you're not qualified to do anything."

For the first time in her life, Karon wanted to punch someone out. She could feel her face flaming, could sense the curious eyes of the park's patrons staring at them. This man is crazy, she thought. No sense arguing with him. Just smile and walk away, don't say another word. And that's just what she did, trembling and furious. Let it slide, find out his name and talk to his boss, she repeated to herself until she was safely out of the public eye.

An hour later Karon was still angry when, with a brisk knock on

196

the first aid door, the same electrician strode in. He had come to see her license, he said. He wanted proof she was a registered nurse, then added that even if she was one she wasn't trained to treat even a finger injury "without an x-ray." For half an hour the man argued with Karon, demanding a list of the kinds of patients she'd treated before, the classes she'd taken, and the number of hours of training she had. "I know nurses are nothing," he said, virtually spitting the words out of his mouth. "I know because I took Emergency Medical Training [one of the requirements for paramedics]." He claimed he'd dropped the course voluntarily—Karon later learned he d flunked out—and anyway, he said, he was making more money now as an electrician than he would as a medic. "We just got a dollar an hour raise and you didn't get anything, did you?" he scoffed as he made his way to the door.

But Karon had the last word. Just as the man let go of the door, Karon yelled out, "How do I know you're an electrician, anyway? Show me your card. Show me your union card, then I'll show you how to change a light bulb." Karon thought she'd made an enemy for life but from then on, she and the electrician became good friends.

That afternoon a teenage boy came in with a nose bleed. Karon worked on him and in 20 minutes sent him off. "Thank God, it's fixed," the boy mumbled on his way out the door. "Don't thank God," she said jokingly. "Thank me."

Then she was off to minister to the stars. Every weekend during the peak season, Fun City put on a show and the entertainers had to be catered to. Sally Rand, Gary "U.S." Bonds, Willie Aames (who, when interviewed on a Chicago talk show, insisted that "his nurse" Karon White Gibson stand up in the audience and be introduced to the viewers), Freddie Cannon, Chris Lemon, Bobby Rydell, Captain Marvell, Anson Williams, David Soul, Mary McGregor—Karon met them all; she treated their headaches, nursed their colds, and listened to their chatter—some light, some dismal. At times she found herself playing bodyguard, fending off the waves of groupies who ached for a piece of a tee shirt or the touch of a sweaty palm.

One night she stood on the sawdust floor of the main arena as far overhead Karl Wallenda stepped lightly onto a taut two-inch wire. All around the nurse were the nervous young ushers commandeered to hold the support ropes for the tightrope. They'd received little training for the event and Karon knew that at least three of them were terrified of the responsibility. At a practice session that afternoon, one had said, "What happens if I drop the rope?" It had been a rhetorical question, but the great Wallenda had overheard. With complete calm he'd looked at the boy. "Then I fall and I die," he said.

Now with the drums rolling and a thousand pairs of eyes stretched upward to the top of the big tent, Karon prayed quietly. "Please don't fall," she said. "Please don't fall." Step by step the grand old man of the high wire act moved over the hushed audience. He was stunning to watch, a real master of a seemingly impossible task. He did not fall; he looked like he never could. Karon applauded until her hands were sore. Several weeks later she would turn cold at the news that Karl Wallenda had taken his last walk through the sky, on a windy, restless day in Puerto Rico.

chapter twelve

*F*or nearly a year Karon and Joy had been searching for a lawyer to handle their suit against General Community Hospital. They were in an awkward position. Yes, they would sue, but no, they didn't know when they could begin the proceedings. This was midsummer, 1977, and they still had no word from the EEOC. Only the determination letter, issued over a year earlier, sat in their files taunting them. "When's your long lost brother, the Right to Sue, going to come join you?" Karon said one day looking through their files; she'd long since given up talking to the EEOC. "It's coming; these things take time," that's all anyone there ever said.

"We want to be ready when the notice does come," Karon had said some fourteen months earlier. "So we have to start, we have to find the best lawyers we can get." There was no question in their minds that they would seek the assistance of a woman attorney; to date, the male lawyers they'd dealt with had all been less than satisfactory. When one had offered, for a $300 fee, to write a letter to the hospital requesting they have their jobs back, Joy had been indignant. "It didn't cost me $300 to get the job the first time," she said. "I'm certainly not going to pay that now to get it back."

The nurses' problem was in locating an attorney who was well-versed in their type of case, and who was willing to take on such a seemingly invincible adversary. Armed with a list of names supplied by a number of different women's organizations, Karon and Joy began making calls. The lawyer they really wanted was a former officer of the Fair Employment Practice Commission now in private practice. She would take the case, she said, but only for a set fee, not on a contingency basis. "We can't afford that," the nurses said, dejected once again. A number of other people turned them down also, pleading overwork and a reluctance to take on new clients. Others declined because of lack of experience in this area. "It's just not our type of case," they'd say. For a while Karon and Joy felt despairing. How many times would they have to endure the old runaround? How much more of it could they take?

Then Karon remembered reading a story about a nurse who was fired for refusing to wear her cap on duty. "Her attorney was a woman and she's the one for us." Except no one could remember the attorney's name. A call to the Illinois Nurses Association didn't help either. "Do you believe they won't tell me who the attorney was because we don't belong to the organization? They gave me her first name, that's all. A lotta good that's going to do." Go ahead, throw up some more brick walls, Karon thought. I love to go smashing my head against them. Let's not have any cooperation, let's just play the old game of making it as hard as possible for each other.

The nurses were eating lunch together discussing the dilemma when their old friend the phone man walked in. By now, the three were accustomed to helping with each other's problems. Bill had barely sat down before Karon began pouring out their latest woe. "Oh, I know who you mean," Bill said, taking a nonchalant bite of a hamburger. "Yeah, neat lady. I took a course from her on law and the private citizen at Glitten College." The nurses didn't even bother to finish their meal. They said something about sending a case of champagne, took the lawyer's name, and ran back to Karon's apartment to call. In a second, their bubble of hope burst around them. The attorney was terribly sorry but she was relocating to another city. Tomorrow would be her last day in Chicago.

"Can you recommend someone else?" Karon asked. No, the woman said, she didn't know any attorneys who were getting involved in these kinds of cases.

200

"Just remember one thing; we can't give up. We are too close to quit." Karon made her voice strong as she talked to her partner, though both wore the same dejected look on their faces.

Finally, in late summer, 1978, Karon and Joy found legal counsel they respected and could trust. Two young women in practice had listened to the nurses talk for long hours, had read the files and papers that had accumulated to date, and had agreed to take the case. The lawyers were up front about their conditions. They would do a thorough character check on Joy and Karon—whatever that meant—to protect themselves. Any irregularities at all and they'd drop the nurses as clients. It was a disturbing feeling, this sense of being on trial but it was one Joy and Karon realized they would have to get used to. "In a sense, I guess, everything we've tried to do is on trial," Karon said to Ralph. "We win or we lose; the practice wins or loses."

All at once events were closing in a heady rush. The nurses had no sooner reached an agreement with the attorneys than the Right to Sue notices arrived. One each for Karon and Joy. An incredible sixteen months after the EEOC determination had been made, almost four years since the original charges had been filed. Finally, when they had almost no patience left, when they had spent their energies, their stores of reserve and nerve, Karon and Joy were given the green light to see their case through. The government could take as long as it pleased in bungling through its paperwork; Joy and Karon now had 90 days to take any action.

This was a surreal time, when days and weeks melted into each other and became one indiscernible blob of memory. Karon and Joy talked to the lawyers; the attorneys filed the suit and talked to the hospital's lawyers; interrogatories were issued in the court and then time extensions granted. One step forward, six back, and three to the side. The legal machinery had been set in motion. Now it would operate at its own pace, chewing up facts, figures, and dates, boring into people's hearts and souls, plodding slowly on.

Through the fall the legal process went, and then on into the spring of 1978. Karon and Joy's nerves were constantly on edge. Every morning began with a question mark, every day ended on the same uncertain note. The case became their lives; it consumed them, ruled them, battered them harshly. The nurses' attorneys called one day with good news: the woman attorney from the Fair Employment Practice Commission, who originally said she would take the case only for a set fee, now was willing to act as a consultant on the case. She would be paid by Joy and Karon's attorneys out of the already agreed-upon fees. There would be no additional legal costs to the nurses for her assistance. She must really believe in us, they thought. It was one bright spot to bolster Karon and Joy's spirits, even as the interminable waiting continued.

Suddenly, a quantum leap forward. Legal depositions were to be taken in the attorneys' offices downtown. With a court reporter taking down every word, the principals were questioned. Three witnesses from the hospital were called to give testimony, then Joy and Karon individually took the stand. All were under oath to tell the truth. Between the two of them, Karon and Joy gave more than 250 pages of testimony. They answered questions going back to the beginning of their employment at General; they were asked about procedures, responsibilities, about past performance, and the events surrounding their dismissal.

The hospital's witnesses were asked similar questions. One, a supervisor, stated that when Karon and Joy were on the psych ward together the department was well run and she never had to worry about it. The person who later took over, she said, was not really qualified. The supervisor also explained that termination resulted if nurses weren't doing their job, if patients complained, or if drugs were missing. The procedure was for a supervisor to submit a written report, then counsel the offender. Three times these steps must be taken and if the performance is still not improved, the person is fired. The witness testified she had never written up anything on Karon or Joy and to her knowledge knew of no one else who had.

Another hospital supervisor said she had had some discussion with Karon long before the dismissal about a minor personnel problem, which she'd never been able to document and hadn't written up until around the time of the firing. She'd done so then, she said, at the request of the Director of Nursing. The director herself testified also, giving a different version from the one Karon and Joy had given about the events involving the dismissal.

The tension surrounding these appearances was incredible. Here in this legal setting, the two nurses found themselves treated on a par with people from whom they'd taken orders before. For hours and days they listened to each other and to the hospital representatives, reliving in their own minds the memories, both good and bad, of another time four years before. They saw themselves now as stronger women, as women who had a new identity. They were not speaking simply as former hospital employees but as independent practitioners, nurses, and businesswomen in their own right, and this sense of identity added strength to their words.

"Were you ever told by [Mrs. T.] or anyone, any other member of the hospital management, that you could not participate in this business outside duty hours or that it was against hospital policy?" Karon was asked.

"Never."

"To your knowledge, was Mrs. Catterson ever told that she could not participate in that business outside duty hours?"

"Never."

When Joy was asked what she thought the dismissal was tied to, she answered succinctly.

"I believe I was terminated for my nursing practice."

"For your 'nursing practice,' what do you mean by that?"

"My Registered Professional Nurses."

"Because of your outside employment?"

"Yes."

Then, as quickly as the spate of activity began, it ended. Joy and Karon were tossed out into the summer air to wait. They'd given their testimony and now their work was finished. The lawyers took over again, promising that someday in a far-off future a court date would be set.

This waiting period was a little easier than the others had been. For one thing, Karon and Joy were confident of the outcome. Despite occasional lapses into panic, and worry about what surprise punches the hospital might throw, they were largely sure of themselves and their case. But there'd been other changes in their lives too, which added to their calm and newly acquired sense of ease.

For one thing Ralph and Karon's custody fight was over, finally, finished that spring. Ralph had been awarded legal rights to Becky, although she was placed under the physical custody of her mother. Not the settlement Karon and Ralph had wanted and fought for, but a compromise they could accept. At least the meetings and counseling sessions and the endless hours at home spent talking about the case were over. The worry and uncertainty about the final decision were removed. For two years Karon had wondered what kind of plans to make—plans for only her and Ralph or plans that would include a teenaged daughter. With Becky gone, Karon felt a personal loss. She'd always liked the girl and thought Becky had a chance for a good future with them.

Karon was bitter over the case; she couldn't deny that. She'd had to listen to accusations that had burned her heart. She'd been forced to watch her husband fight a battle he could not win. She'd spent months asking herself why, analyzing everything she knew about Becky's life, all to no avail. There were no answers, she decided, only solutions and quirks of fate, and this was the solution imposed on them. "Maybe we can get back to our perpetual date now," Karon said to Ralph, when they finally got home.

As for Joy, her wedding ring was back on her left hand. There were times she felt almost like a new bride, distracted by the shiny gold band, pleased by the feel of the metal against her skin. The old Gordon she'd fought with and ignored for so long had disappeared into the ozone the previous year. He'd stopped drinking and then eight months later had started running. Suddenly Joy realized this *was* the man she'd married, an easygoing, entertaining, caring man. This was the Gordon she'd dreamed of, not an uncommunicative body snoring on the couch, but a man who was genuinely interested in her, in their family, in life. Gordon, who hadn't cared about anything for years, was now the Little League father of the neighborhood, attending games and working on the field on his days off. He got involved with a policeman's group, became a listener for his wife's stories and adventures, graduated into a marathon runner. He even started to take Spanish lessons—to help with his work, he explained. Joy could not find the words to tell Gordon of her new pride in him. She put on his wedding ring and let it speak for her.

Like a puzzle, the pieces of life were falling quietly into place for Karon and Joy. Only one piece remained out of line. It towered over the horizon, but it was only one piece and someday soon it would topple and a decade would be completed. For it was exactly ten years before that Karon and Joy had met, that their paths had begun winding together, forming the personal and professional bonds that had allowed them to challenge the ordinary and break the molds that for long had defined their lives as nurses and women. They'd won all their battles so far, had learned and grown along the way. They were ready for the big one. There was no turning back, no sidestepping the issue. They would wait—that was all.

*   *   *   *   *

The summer following the taking of the depositions was a "yes, but" period for Karon and Joy. Yes, they were sure they'd win. Yes, they were glad they'd stuck it out and gone this far. Yes, the future looked promising. But, what if they lost? Theoretically, the decision should not affect their professional standing, although in practice Karon and Joy knew it would. As matters stood, they might never get a decent reference from General. That black blot of being fired would always loom in the background. Before, when they'd tried to get a loan for an old people's center the financier had turned them down simply because they were nurses. What if they wanted to try again, to borrow money for the business, what chance would they have as nurses with a "bad record"?

Psychologically, losing to the hospital would devastate the two women. The fight symbolized everything to them. They still believed in nursing, despite the problems, the ups and downs, but could they go on believing if they lost this battle? Both Karon and Joy were reluctant to discuss their plans but each had secretly thought of leaving the profession entirely. Breaking away, making a clean sweep, and just walking out. The idea of quitting haunted them, as if they feared that losing their case would make it inevitable.

All summer they tried not to discuss the case but found they could talk about little else. Their lives were in a strange limbo; everything seemed qualified, to be pending, to lack definition.

When the final action began, it came like a thunderbolt. Karon got the call in early October; the court date was set, she was told, for five days from then. The lawyers needed to talk to them, could they come in the next day? Karon and Joy needed to talk again to each other. They suddenly had to retell the entire story, the story they'd lived for years. Karon talked to Ralph, for whatever advice and assurance he could give. Joy needed to talk to Gordon, for support and encouragement. They talked to get over this final waiting period; they talked because they could hardly wait for this final showdown.

Suddenly, there was a change in plans. The hospital wanted to settle, quietly, without the hubbub and publicity of a public hearing. Could they all meet just before the court date? The atmosphere in the room was electric. Attorneys for General assumed the nurses would be easy targets. But Joy and Karon balked at the offering. To them the biggest bone of contention was reputation: they must have in writing an agreement that the hospital would not deny their good records. They must have a guarantee of reference letters that gave full credit to their years of faithful service. They insisted the hospital say that they had left in good standing. General's lawyers were put in an uproar.

"Be reasonable," they said.

"We *are* being reasonable," Karon replied. "This is our lives we're dealing with." All the years of being a good nurse, of taking orders, all the hundreds of times she and Joy had worked their tails off for General, all the pride they'd taken in the place. Then the humiliation, the flippant disregard for them, the insinuation that to be a real nurse you had to be one of their nurses. These thoughts were behind the words that Karon laid out carefully and with finality.

Then for two days they went back and forth in a continued series of phone calls, until finally at 5:00 P.M. of the afternoon before the court date Joy and Karon came to a unanimous decision: either the hospital attorneys agree to their stipulations about their references and records or the nurses would see them in court. They were ready to fight and the hospital knew it.

Soon after, it was all over. Settled out of court. Karon and Joy had seen their fight through and had come out on top. The hospital agreed to their demands. The terminations would be deleted from their records. Their files would indicate they had left in good standing. If Karon or Joy wanted references from General, they would be given top marks, reflecting their years of honorable service. The hospital also came up with a financial settlement acceptable to the two women, insisting only that certain specifics (including money amounts) not be disclosed by either party, an arrangement Karon and Joy were willing to compromise on. To them, money wasn't the major issue. From the beginning they were concerned primarily with clearing their names and protecting their professional status. The two little girls who'd dreamed of nursing, the two grown women who'd dedicated their lives to this calling.

"We showed them," they agreed. "We proved our point." Somehow these two, these women who were "just nurses," like someone might be "just" a housewife or "just" a bus driver, these two from the side of life where you didn't ask questions and only listened to the wisdom and direction of the experts, the better educated, the better connected, these people who were supposed to accept their roles as cogs in the larger wheel of life—they had triumphed. They'd penetrated the giant, crazy maze of the legal and bureaucratic world and refused to be sidetracked or intimidated. They had stood up for their rights and what they believed in and they'd remained standing even as the powerful and the established had tried to sit on them.

Karon and Joy had gained success for themselves, a victory for the nursing profession. They were exonerated and had legitimized the independent practitioner.

Now, time to get back to the real business, the practice of nursing. Call realtors and begin again to plot the reopening of their office; call and write more letters to expand their services. They'd talked about opening a summer office in Lake Geneva, a Wisconsin resort town; maybe this was the time to look into that possibility more seriously. With the cloud gone from the future, they could plan now, determine exactly what direction they wanted to go in and plot out the steps carefully and confidently.

One thing was for certain: hospital nursing, once the only phase of their profession they'd known, was light-years behind them. They'd never go back, not to General nor to any other hospital. Life would be easier that way but Karon and Joy no longer looked for what was easy. They wanted what was different. A year from now they'd be working on a movie set at the elegant Ambassador East Hotel; they'd be at the historic Palmer House discussing the takeover of a large-scale home nursing service with a group of oil-rich Texans; they would still be plotting their options and hanging their hopes on the one small dream that had started it all, an innocent part-time independent practice in a little out-of-the-way office.

Joy and Karon felt good going out to dinner that night. How many hours had they put in like this, behind the wheel tooling off toward the unknown? It would be impossible to count them all, ten years' worth of experiences stretching across a horizon that was painful to tread at times but never boring. They'd had fun along the way too, and plenty of laughs. They'd had moments of despair, then wonderful exhilarating times when they conquered a new challenge. Each was proud right now and pleased that she could bring home news her husband and family would be proud of.

When they'd started the practice they'd both been able to say, "We did it." The thrill of that moment had never left them. And now the feeling was strengthened—they had done the right thing. Their dream hadn't been all that cockeyed.

"I really don't think I could have done it differently," Karon remarked to her partner. She knew that blind faith in her own abilities had made her persist when it would have been so easy to give up. She had earned every bit of her success and had gained so much along the way. From the independent practice and all that ensued came professional growth; because of the association with Joy she'd discovered a lighter, more gentle side to her personality. No regrets, thought Karon, no regrets at all.

Joy had her shiny brown hair brushed back over her shoulders. She was beaming. Who would ever have thought she would be here today celebrating this kind of victory? Ten years before Joy herself would have scoffed at the idea. She was a different woman today sitting in that car. She liked that, the feeling that one could change and grow even as an adult. Ten years ago Joy assumed she had reached a pinnacle, established the pattern that would be her entire life. How wrong I was, she thought. How much more you can be if you try.

* * * * *

A few months later, Joy and Karon appeared on a Chicago radio show, espousing the role of the independent nurse practitioner. A third guest on the program was a physician who admitted he knew nothing about nurses practicing on their own. For five minutes prior to air time, Karon and Joy bombarded the man with details and information; during the broadcast they outlined their procedures and goals and talked eloquently of the need for such a service.

The physician became an instant convert to their cause. As the three of them left the studio, following the 30-minute broadcast the doctor mused quietly to himself, then turned to the two women. "You know what you are?" he said. "You're like two modern-day Joan of Arcs."

Driving home after the settlement—lost in their private thoughts and the shocklike aftereffects of their experience—Karon and Joy didn't realize it at the time, couldn't have put it into the words the doctor would later use, but that's what they felt like.

"Two modern-day Joan of Arcs."

chapter thirteen

*T*he autumn of 1978 was one of the best ever for Karon and Joy. They were suddenly beyond a legal battle that had hung over their heads for five years, that had occupied half their time and a good deal of their energies. But what do to now? They wanted to reopen an office but just couldn't do it in the way they had the first time around. They had accumulated too much business know-how to make the old mistakes again. They wanted to further advance their nursing careers only they weren't sure how or where.

The uncertainty didn't bother them because, through all their ordeals, both Karon and Joy had retained a firm faith in themselves and an innocent belief that all things would work out in the end.

That fall, the two took a little time to relax and enjoy themselves. They spent time at the cottage in Lake Geneva, Wisconsin, that Karon had recently bought. They talked about their plans and decided not to rush headlong into any one venture. They would bide their time as the future rolled toward them.

The first thing the future dumped on the two women was snow. Mountains of it, frozen over by record-freezing low temperatures, the snow stopped the entire city in its tracks. The nurse practitioners had started daydreaming again of hanging out their shingle just before the worst winter in history began.

For almost three months, Karon, Joy and the six million other people in their city struggled merely to survive and get through the day-to-day hassles of living in an ice kingdom. Getting a car out of a garage was considered a major accomplishment that winter, completing a normal half-hour drive in two to three hours was about a par for the course. Even an independent nursing practice had to bow to the forces of nature. This was, after all, the snow that would close down the world's busiest airport and open up the door for Jane Byrne to be elected Chicago's first woman mayor, one of the biggest political upsets in the city's history.

"I'm going to get Byrne to campaign out here, " Karon announced one day. "She's bucking the system, the same as we tried, by speaking out and I want to help her." Unfortunately, the mayoral candidate's speaking calendar was already filled. "Why don't you have her ride on a dog sled—that'd be a great campaign gimmick," Karon suggested to Byrne's manager, but he demurred. "You ride the sled and pass out literature," he countered. No way, thought Karon, it won't be effective. And the nurses turned back to nursing.

As independent practitioners, Karon and Joy continued to staff the recovery unit at a local abortion clinic through the winter; they still managed a few insurance physicals each week; and they were able to complete an occasional house call, but that was all. They couldn't even make it to two scheduled TV interviews. With the coming of spring, however, things began popping.

One sunny day, they received a call from a medical supplier who was looking to expand into the nursing business. He offered to buy Registered Professional Nurses. Absolutely not, Karon and

Joy said. They were flattered by the proposal but couldn't imagine giving up what they'd worked so hard to establish. "Well, if you want to be honest, if someone offered us a million dollars, I'd probably be swayed," Joy mused on their way back from an insurance physical one Sunday afternoon. "But it would have to be plenty for all we've been through." Karon agreed; she was already making contingency plans in case such a fabulous event occurred. "We could always start a new practice, though I don't think we'd ever come up with a name I like so much and I'd really hate to lose our logo."

The nurses didn't talk about selling the business again, not that day. They had too much else to discuss; first a news report that a former patient from the psych ward had been found gunned down gangland style ("We treated a mafia man!" Joy exclaimed, "Make a good title for a book," said Karon); then the gossip that an old pharmacist friend had been indicted for illegal drug traffic; and the discovery that General Community Hospital was, in fact, sending out references that reflected their years of good service (Karon had had a call about her Chicago Police department application and was pleased to hear the interviewer comment on her "excellent references").

As always, for the independent nurse practitioners, life continued full of surprises, both large and small. The funniest was the legal notice informing them a former patient from their practice had gone into bankruptcy; he owed them a total of $10.00 and they would be paid $2.00 per month until the debt was cleared. "Shall we order the Rolls?" Joy asked. "Think we can afford one now that we've come into all this money?"

Later, an associate nurse called after completing a home visit for Registered Professional Nurses. "Meet me at Roditis' in Greek town in ten minutes," she told Karon. "I hope you don't mind but I'll be wearing blue jeans." Karon exploded. "Blue jeans to see a patient in?" The nurse defended herself, said the woman insisted she mow the lawn as part of her services. "Looks like we're going to have to rethink our policies and spell them out for our associates and patients," Karon said to Joy. "Imagine a nurse cutting grass on a house call."

Patient care policies weren't all Karon and Joy had to reconsider. One day, they learned that the abortion clinic where they worked in the recovery unit might have to close its doors. The physician owner was livid and promised that if the local government started to question the clinic's license, he would take the matter into court.

"When did all this come out?" Joy asked Karon.

"Yesterday."

"Great. And how long before it's supposed to be decided?"

"Next week."

"Gives us just loads of time to decide what to do, doesn't it?"

Only they didn't need much time. In one afternoon, they made up their minds. Their nursing licenses meant too much to risk losing. Karon and Joy had never done anything illegal, and they weren't going to take any chances now. Effective immediately, Registered Professional Nurses terminated its agreement with the clinic.

Then in early summer, Karon and Joy learned that their counterparts on the other side of the city had sold their business to another nurse. "She's a master's degree RN, used to work at a state prison – I don't know," Karon told Joy. They were both two-year diploma nurses and had had enough of the professional nursing organizations preaching against RNs like themselves and advocating instead a push for more nurses with advanced degrees. Still, they called the woman, extended the olive branch, offered to share their experiences and discovered they really liked her. They would, they all agreed, get together that summer and talk.

Shortly afterward, in mid-July, Karon got one of those phone calls that always catches the recipient slightly off guard. It was from the Illinois Film Office, a department Karon had contacted months before and had long since given up any hope of ever hearing from. The office was, she knew, the liaison between local interests and Hollywood producers.

"There are two movies going to be made in the Chicago area and I gave your names to both companies, if that's all right with you," the voice on the phone said. "One of the films is for something called *My Bodyguard*. There'll be a lot of teenagers used as extras and they need someone to watch over these kids. I know it's kind of unusual, but do you think your nurses would mind?"

Karon assured the caller that unusual or not, her nurses wouldn't mind at all. "Who can I call about this?" she asked.

"Oh, they'll call you."

Right, thought Karon, just like the cow will jump over the moon.

But a week later, the assistant production manager did call and, after hearing a quote on fees, gave Registered Professional Nurses the job.

Suddenly, Karon and Joy, who'd been psych nurses and med-surg nurses, pediatrics nurses, emergency room nurses, orthopedic nurses and industrial nurses, became "location nurses." They began to toss around terms like *honey wagon* and *crew call sheets* and *wrap* and *take* and *retake*. They started hobnobbing with directors, producers, and even teenage movie stars. Not that the job was all glory. Work days – six days a week – ran a minimum of ten hours, sometimes a maximum of fourteen.

215

After an initial two weeks on one set location, the nurses and their associates found themselves moving daily from one neighborhood to another. The actors and production people were chauffeured from hotel to location. The nurses, who were local, had to hustle around town on their own, with never more than twelve hours notice on where they'd be working next.

Karon and Joy felt privileged on the job. They were treated well and invited to share in the fabulous feed spread Hollywood caterers put out every day. But, still, in subtle ways they were reminded of lesser status for "nurse." On the first day of filming, for example, the associate nurse they'd sent on the assignment had to sit all day in a bee-filled Lincoln Park cafeteria and dash in and out through the rain to the set whenever she was needed. "No way," Karon told the production manager the next day, and only then was Registered Professional Nurses given its own honey wagon room – a portable dressing room complete with lavatory, couch, lighted mirror, director's chair, and sink, set in a converted trailer truck. Everyone affiliated with the movie had rooms in honey wagons, Karon pointed out, why not the nurse?

Then, midway through the project, the producer and the director scheduled a Sunday afternoon boat outing on Lake Michigan. The teamsters who drove the honey wagon trucks, the actors and all the production people received invitations. Of the four nurses involved with the movie, only Karon was asked to the party (later, she found, because she was the business contact for Registered Professional Nurses). Karon called the production office and said she wanted the other nurses invited as well. She felt relieved when the entire event was cancelled – everyone had wanted to bring a guest and there wasn't enough room.

But Karon's crusading paid off. When shooting transferred to the Ambassador East Hotel, the nurses were allotted a portion of a deluxe 14th Floor suite for their first aid station. They had to share the space with wardrobe, and the rest of the suite with production, makeup, and hair dressing, but no one complained. The setting was definitely comfortable if a bit crowded. At the end of the two-week hotel stint, director Tony Bill hosted a party in the Dimensions Lounge, adjacent to the famous Pump Room, and this time all the nurses were invited. The walls around them were covered with celebrity photos of Hollywood stars who'd sat in the prestigious booth number one. Chitchatting and shaking hands were the stars of the ongoing film – Ruth Gordon, John Houseman, Martin Mull. Hospital nursing was never like this.

Karon and Joy expected working the movies to be exciting. And though they experienced boring hours of sitting through a dozen takes of the same shot, there were other moments when all heck could break loose and any number of mishaps occur.

The storyline of the movie lent itself to disaster. It revolved around a sheltered. wealthy boy (Chris Makepeace) who attended a rough and tough urban school where gangs proliferated and were notorious for extracting "protection" money from other students. The rich kid decides that rather than pay the extortion charges, he'll hire the meanest kid in the school to be his bodyguard. The boy who qualifies for the slot supposedly killed his own brother, which is about as mean as one can get.

The plot lent itself to hectic chase scenes, wild motorcycle rides and other types of mayhem in the seedier neighborhoods of the city. One day, for example, Karon began her morning at a mammoth truck and junkyard in the light industrial zone that rings the southern edge of the downtown. Looking in one direction Karon could see the city skyline pristine against the morning light; off to another side and more immediate was an Amtrak repair station with trains moving in and out of a long

217

series of old wooden sheds. Behind her were trucks, hundreds of them it seemed, lined up like steel nosed beetles ready for an attack. Off to the other side was a huge crushing machine, busy smashing junk cars and other vehicles into cookie sheets. And here we are with a bunch of kids, one of whom is bound to get rolled over or smashed or cut a finger or get lockjaw, Karon thought. Incredibly, the crew made it safely out of the yard. They spent the rest of the morning in a special van, following the rich kid and the bodyguard on a motorcycle drive through nearby streets. At one point, the director, who was riding along atop a station wagon "keeping a low profile" as one of the assistant directors teased, was considering trying to film the two riders zipping across a track in front of an approaching train. But the idea was dropped.

The most potentially hazardous shoot was made with both Karon and Joy on location. It was planned as a typical after-school scene, with a couple of hundred teenagers racing out the front door of the high school, running through the school yard and dashing across the street, just like kids do. Except no one driving down the street expected a stampede of two hundred shouting students to appear from nowhere in the middle of August. Worse yet, the scene was shot at 4 PM, already the height of evening rush hour. "We want it to look real," the kids were told. "Just run out there and ignore the traffic."

More than anything, it was this lack of staging that surprised Karon and Joy. They thought every step, every tiny detail was worked out in advance, that every car and face appearing in a scene was deliberately set in place. Movie making, in reality, was much more spontaneous than the nurses had expected. Still, in all, despite the random nature of the process and the sometimes almost carefree manner in which various stunts were arranged, no one was ever hurt. With one exception: during the filming inside the school, a crewmember tripped on a camera cord, fell and broke his nose.

Grueling work, Karon and Joy called their movie business, but they loved it and were busy finding out how to get more film assignments, even as they coped with other developments. For one, their meetings with the city's other independent nurse practitioner were leading toward a possible new business arrangement, in which Karon and Joy would either share her office or the three would join forces and start up a triple practice in yet another area of Chicago. Then there were the Texas people. Karon had spotted their ad in the Sunday paper, something about nurses needed to run a health-service agency. "Those are the people we talked with two years ago," she told Joy. "I'm going to find out what's going on with them." Karon talked to a woman who claimed her correspondence with Registered Professional Nurses had never been answered. "That's because we never got your letter," Karon explained. "Well, if you're still interested," the woman said, "so are we."

The Texas group operated a number of offices in various cities that tried to provide on a large scale some of the services Karon and Joy offered through their independent practice. The firm needed someone reliable to head up its Chicago branch, had been impressed with the two independent practitioners the first time around and wanted to negotiate. That was on a Tuesday. The following week, the president and vice president would be coming in from Dallas to meet with Joy and Karon. The nurses wanted to contract through their business for the job; the Texas people said *No, we might want to buy you out, then hire you to operate our agency.* But first, the company wanted to see their books; could they bring them in the next day? Too fast,

219

Karon and Joy said, just hold up a minute. The nurses weren't sure they wanted anyone to see their accounts; they wanted to talk to other business people they knew, confer with their lawyer, think about the arrangement.

The next day, on their way to the movie location, they discussed their sudden blossoming of options. "I remember when we didn't have very many," Joy said. "This sure is a pleasant change of pace, couldn't have happened to two nicer people." The nurse practitioners had the possible collaboration with the other nurse, a woman they both admired and respected, to think about; the Texas arrangement to consider; maybe more movie deals coming down the pike. Plus two other biggies up their sleeve. The Pope was coming to Chicago in what was developing as the event of the century. Registered Professional Nurses might help staff the downtown first aid stations for the two-day celebration. "Nurses to the Pope," quipped Joy, the agnostic. "I can't believe it." Also, Karon had written to Chicago Mayor Jane Byrne, citing a number of area health service problems the press had recently uncovered and offering Registered Professional Nurses' expertise on a consulting basis. *We're the people who wanted to put you on a dog sled during your campaign*, she wrote. "That should catch someone's attention," she told Joy.

On their morning drive through the city, both women exuded a comfortable confidence. Even if the worst came about and none of their immediate plans worked out, they weren't worried. They'd always have other ideas, other plans in their newfound arsenal of almost limitless possibilities.

In eleven years of dreaming and working together, Karon Gibson and Joy Catterson had discovered that they had the power to shape their own lives. They didn't have to accept the cards they'd been dealt. In establishing themselves as independent

220

nurse practitioners, they had grabbed hold of fate and molded it to their own purpose. In the many trials that had ensued, they had earned something, and that was the privilege of not being afraid to face the new and different.

As the two women barreled off together into the first hours of a seeming endless parade of tomorrows, they knew they could not predict what awaited them. But that was all right, because they were sure of one thing, completely and assuredly.

The future belonged to them.

Epilogue

*I*n April 1980, Karon Gibson and Joy Catterson reopened their independent nurse practitioner office on the south side of Chicago. Business was brisk from the start.

Less than a year later, *Nurses: On Our Own* was published. The book detailed both Karon and Joy's struggle to establish themselves as independent nurse practitioners and their legal fight with their hospital employer. As part of the book's publicity campaign, the two women appeared on radio and television interview programs throughout the Midwest. Their story also was featured in local and national magazines.

Although everything was going well for the two nurses, circumstances were once again about to shift. As her four children grew up, Joy found it increasingly difficult to balance the challenge of raising a family with the long, irregular hours and financial uncertainty of running their own small business. With a heavy heart, Joy left the business, though not the profession. She needed flexibility and found it in a variety of nursing positions that carried her through the present. Today, along with a new partner, Joy once again operates an independent, specialized nursing service.

Left to run the office of Registered Professional Nurses alone, Karon continued to provide home-based health care to families throughout the city and to expand her work in movies. Over the course of five years, her office provided First Aid Services for *Dr. Detroit*, starring Dan Akroyd, *Risky Business* with Tom Cruise, *Naked Face* with Roger Moore and *Bad Boys* featuring Sean Penn. On the set of the TV movie, *Conspiracy of Love*, she even tended to Robert Young, the well-known TV doc of *Marcus Welby* and *Father Knows Best* fame.

Determined to prove her business acumen, Karon also took over the helm of a struggling company that provided private duty and home nursing services. The firm was nearly bankrupt when Karon came on board. She stabilized the operation, then began to open more offices. Soon, the firm had four successful offices in the metropolitan area. In 1987, Karon established AmericaNurse, Ltd, another independent nursing business which she headed up. The firm provided homecare private duty nursing services, occupational health services to major corporations and first aid to the entertainment industry, working on the sets of locally produced TV commercials. Clients included ads for Mike Ditka's Grabowskis, the Johnson and Johnson Company and various other corporations.

Karon's many efforts did not go unnoticed.

In spring of 1982, Karon was named Business Woman of the Year by the Chicago Chapter of the National Association of Women in Business. In summer of 1984, Arthur Anderson and Company honored her with the Small Business of the Year Award. The following year, in 1985, the daily Southtown Newspaper named Karon as its Woman of the Year for her business skills and community activism. Karon also was invited to join the Committee of 200, a group of preeminent business owners and corporate executives. As a member, she attended Executive Management seminars at Harvard, the University of

Chicago and the University of Pennsylvania's Wharton School of Business.

Through the 1980s, Karon provided care for more than one thousand patients. When patients found their benefits threatened by former employers and government agencies, Karon went to bat for them. She cut through bureaucratic red tape and took businesses to court, often arguing the patients' cases herself. During this period, Karon employed hundreds of nurses, in many instances offering part-time employment to women who had dropped out of the profession to raise their children. Determined to generate greater awareness and public recognition for the nursing profession, she even created the Chicagoland Nurse of the Year Award.

Despite her dedication to the nursing profession, Karon realized she had another calling. On the book tour for *Nurses: On Our Own*, Karon got her first taste of appearing in front of a TV camera. She enjoyed the work so much, she soon began to produce and host a 15 minute TV program called *Healthbreak*. From 1982 to 1987, the show aired on cable TV stations in both Chicago and Palm Beach, Florida. Before long, Karon realized she wanted to devote full-time to providing television viewers with shows that focused on health and safety issues. It took several years for Karon to fully realize her dream. First, she had to ensure that former patients and nurse employees were provided for. At the same time, she had to cultivate markets and sell cable providers on her ideas. One of her favorite programs is a one hour special on street safety that she developed with her policeman husband Ralph and his partner Investigator Gil Broderick.

Currently, Karon has several shows to her credit. She is cohost of *Senior Connection* and producer and host for both the *Karon Gibson Show* and *Outspoken With Karon*. The three shows are broadcast on cable and educational stations in Illinois and Florida.

Today, after years of working long, arduous hours, Karon enjoys the luxury of dividing her time between homes in Chicago and Wisconsin and wintering in Palm Beach, where she relaxes and tapes many of her shows. Thanks to the financial freedom she gained from her various nursing ventures, Karon is able to devote her time and energy to the two activities she enjoys most: educating the public about important health issues and meeting innovative and interesting people every day.

Karon will never forget where it all started. Personal and professional success, she says, evolved from the challenges she faced and the economic freedom she gained through an independent practice in nursing.